To - Gary

Fro[m] ... 1998.

Happy Birthday

x x x

RED ARROWS
A Year in the Life

RED ARROWS
A Year in the Life

THE OFFICIAL STORY

TONY CUNNANE   Photographs by CHRIS BENNETT

ANDRE
DEUTSCH

Dedicated to Joan Harris Bennett,
who died 15 April 1997

First published in Great Britain in 1997
by André Deutsch Ltd
106 Great Russell Street London WC1B 3LJ
André Deutsch is a subsidiary of VCI plc

A catalogue record for this title is available from the British Library

ISBN 0 233 99119 0

Book design by Design 23

Colour reproduction by Dot Gradations England.

Printed and bound in Italy by Vincenzo Bona, Turin

Foreword

The Royal Air Force Aerobatic Team has entertained countless millions of fans since it was formed in 1965 and has become a national institution with an unparalleled international reputation. If anyone, almost anywhere in the world, mentions the name Red Arrows, there is no need to explain who or what they are. I have watched the Team in action every year and, in 1967, had the pleasure of flying with them – or, to be more precise, I flew one practice sortie in Ray Hanna's back seat. Since 1989 I have had the honour of being the Red Arrows' full-time Public Relations Officer. Whenever I watch the Team in action, in practice or in public, I do so with pride and awe. The Team not only represents the 'Best of British', it really does fly the flag for the United Kingdom.

For some years now I have wanted to tell the story of what goes on behind the scenes. I knew from the thousands of letters and telephone calls I have received while in this job that there is a great thirst for knowledge about the Team and the story of the first year in a new Team Leader's tour seemed a good way to satisfy this demand. I thought it was important to tell the story using the actual words and thoughts of the Team members and the various senior officers who feature in the book. If I have misquoted any of them, or misrepresented official thinking, the fault is mine alone.

Chris Bennett, who has produced the superb photographs which illustrate this book, and I have probably tried the patience of pilots and ground crew alike during the last 12 months but, like the true professionals they are, everyone has responded willingly to our every request, and for that we thank them all.

Prelude

The end of the Royal Air Force Aerobatic Team's 1996 UK flying season was marked by an event that was most unusual even by Red Arrows' standards. Out on their home airfield at the Royal Air Force College, Cranwell in Lincolnshire, a man stood all alone, clutching a thick red book under his arm, staring into the distance and occasionally glancing down at his watch. Had you been able to look closely, you would have thought that he was talking to himself but he was, in fact, talking into a radio microphone and looking directly into the telephoto lens

'Look, on time to the second!' Squadron Leader Tony Cunnane enthusiastically exclaims, pointing to his watch. Exactly on time, the Red Arrows execute a colourful and spectacular Vixen Break for the This Is Your Life *television cameras.*

of a television camera some hundred metres away.

Exactly on cue, the Red Arrows appeared from the Sleaford direction in Vixen formation and performed a spectacular break, each aircraft pulling sharply upwards at a different angle to give a fan-like effect. The man with the book, who had his back to the low-flying aircraft, ducked in surprise that was only partially feigned. Like the good professional that he is, he continued to talk to camera. As the British Aerospace Hawk aircraft passed overhead, the Rolls-Royce Adour jet engines created their own distinctive noise, known as a 'whoosh' to Red Arrows' cognoscenti, which temporarily drowned out all other sounds on the airfield.

A few minutes later the world's premier aerobatic display team landed on their home runway, taxied in close formation towards the flight line, stopped with their nose wheels exactly on the designated spots painted on the tarmac and simultaneously shut down their engines. On a radio signal from the Leader, nine aircraft canopies opened, one after the other, in the form of a Mexican wave. The man with the book, now closely followed by the television cameraman, approached the Team Leader's aircraft.

A sizeable crowd swarmed around the lead aircraft, jostling shoulder to shoulder as briefed earlier by the television director so that the Team Leader would not see the man with the book until everything was ready. In addition to the Red Arrows' blue-suited ground crew there was a motley collection of Station personnel who had left their place of work to watch what was happening. TV camera, sound and lighting technicians burdened with the paraphernalia of their profession, assistant directors and location managers clutching clipboards and mobile phones, all with specific tasks to perform, elbowed their way into postion. The red-suited pilots quickly exited their Hawks and joined the throng. Finally there was a man in a standard issue green flying suit who climbed slowly down from the rear cockpit of the Leader's aircraft and then stayed furtively in the background. Everyone apart from Red Leader knew what was about to happen and they all wanted to hear Michael Aspel, the man with the book, announce, 'Squadron Leader John Rands OBE, this is your life.'

Three weeks later, at midnight on 19 October 1996 in the RAF College bar, the officers of the Red Arrows and their 140 distinguished guests were just beginning to unwind after a superb dinner, fine wines and several lengthy speeches. The occasion was the annual End of Season Guest Night and the guests included the Chief of the Air Staff, former Team members, and many senior executives from the companies that support the RAF Aerobatic Team. The Red Arrows were celebrating the end of their most spectacular, most successful season ever. Between the very first display in May 1965, at RAF Little Rissington in the Cotswolds, and the final display of 1996 in Malta, 102 Red Arrows' pilots had flown a grand total of 3,134 displays in 50 different countries. The tally for the last season alone included 115 displays in 20 different countries across four continents.

Although there was no special ceremony, everyone was aware of the exact time but few would admit to it. Midnight at the End of Season Guest Night marks the end of one Red Arrows' year and the start of another. It is the precise moment when departing members of the Team cease to be Red Arrows and the new pilots formally become Red Arrows.

One of the four new pilots for the 33rd season was the man in the green flying suit who had remained in the background three weeks earlier. During the recording of the television programme later that day, that same man had appeared on stage in formal RAF uniform amidst the current Red Arrows, who were dressed in their conspicuous bespoke red flying suits. John Rands' story was almost told when the cameras settled on the new pilot. Michael Aspel turned to him and said, 'Squadron Leader Simon Meade, you are the next Leader of the Red Arrows. A hard act to follow. How will you do it?'

A Hard Act to Follow

'There were three of us on the short list for the Leader's job,' said Simon on his first day in his new office. 'We each had an interview with a two-star air marshal. My interview was 18 months ago at Laarbruch in Germany where I was Flight Commander on Number 4 Harrier Squadron. That was the first time any two-star had come to me rather than the other way round. It was a 40-minute grilling and I came out of it thinking I'd done very badly, but a week later I got a call to tell me the job was mine. I've been waiting quite a long time since that interview, but now the waiting is over and I'm here.'

The Red Arrows were formed in 1965 but military formation flying and even formation aerobatics go back almost 50 years before that – even before the establishment of the RAF itself, in 1918. From the very earliest

It's October 1996 and Squadron Leader Simon Meade, the new 'Boss', pre-flight briefs the three 'FNGs' – the new pilots on the squadron – prior to their first taste of formation flying, Reds style.

days pilots have always enjoyed demonstrating their skills and their machines in public, but they do so neither to show off, nor solely for their own pleasure. RAF pilots fly in formation so that they can give each other mutual protection in combat; they are taught to fly aerobatics because that form of flying requires pilots to operate their aircraft at, and sometimes beyond, the airframe limits. The RAF has always insisted that its pilots should be able

to fly their aircraft for maximum performance. When two pilots are engaged in combat, flying aircraft of similar performance, it is the better pilot that wins the battle.

All the pilots in the Red Arrows' first few seasons, when the Team was based at Kemble in the Cotswolds, were flying instructors; in fact they were flying instructors' instructors. The Squadron was formed at the RAF's Central Flying School (CFS), the oldest flying school in the world, dating back to 1912. One of the main roles of CFS, then and now, is to train flying instructors. The pilots no longer have to be instructors, although several of them are, but the RAF Aerobatic Team remains functionally part of CFS which now has its headquarters

On 15 October 1996, Simon Meade leads his three 'apprentice' Red Arrows in a formation take off from RAF Cranwell, the Arrows' home base. The jets will not practice overhead Cranwell, but will fly to nearby Scampton – their old home, now officially closed – and utilise the airspace there. As the four-ship departs, below them the yellow vehicle belongs to the bird scarer, whose job it is to dissuade such feathered creatures from loitering about the airfield. A bird down a jet engine intake or a high speed impact can result in dramatic consequences – as one of the new pilots was later to discover.

With nose wheel chocks firmly in place, Cubes prepares to vacate the front office of his British Aerospace Hawk, the look on his always expressive face only hinting at the extreme effort and concentration required for such precision formation aerobatics – particularly when new at it! New to the Red Arrows he might be, but, at 34, Andy Cubin is an old hand at both fast jet and display flying.

collocated with the Red Arrows at Cranwell.

'How do you become a Red Arrow?' is the question most asked by members of the public when they get an opportunity to speak to one of the pilots. Well, it is not easy: the qualifications are daunting and the competition intense. In stark CV terms, before pilots can even be considered for selection they must have completed at least one tour on an operational fast jet aircraft such as the Harrier, Jaguar or Tornado, have been assessed as above average in that role, and be recommended by their Station Commander. Those qualifications might, just *might*, get a pilot on to the annual short list drawn up from 40 or so applicants. But, unlike any other job in the RAF, new Red Arrows' pilots are finally selected from the short list by current Red Arrows' pilots. In other words, it is not so much what you have done but whom you have got to know whilst doing it. This may seem nepotistic, but a degree of personal knowledge and trust is absolutely essential before any pilot will allow another to fly head on to them at 800 miles an hour.

'When will there be a female Red Arrow?' is the question most often asked by female members of the public. For the time being that question is easy for the RAF to answer, 'When there is at least one female applicant with the appropriate qualifications – but so far none has achieved them.' Ask a current Red Arrow the same question and he is likely to answer chauvinistically, but accurately, 'Not in my time anyway!'

Many pilots, particularly those who have no aspiration to join and those who have never met a Red Arrow, have over the years tended to disparage the Team and the pilots, sometimes in the form of friendly banter, sometimes unequivocally. Some label them as prima donnas, an unfortunate term for an all-male team; others see them as poseurs. It is only when you get to know these pilots that you realise they are first amongst unequals and that posing is an essential part of their duties.

To have your name included on the very short list of pilots qualified to become the Red Arrows' Team Leader, a pilot must first have completed a full tour as a Team member and ideally have flown as the Leader of the Synchro Pair, the second-half soloists, in his third and final year. Unlike leaders and top executives in other walks of life where hands-on experience is not always essential, to have credibility as Leader of the Red Arrows you must be able to demonstrate that you can fly all the most demanding positions yourself. Additionally, Red Leader must be of Squadron Leader rank because he is Squadron Commander – Boss – for almost 100 officers and ground crew. The Boss is ultimately responsible for everything that happens on his squadron, from dealing with minor disciplinary matters to discussions with senior officers on higher policy. These minimum qualifications are sensible and ensure that the short list for this unique appointment consists of a very select group of pilots.

Simon Meade is well qualified in every respect for one of the most prominent, glamorous and rewarding flying jobs in the RAF. He joined the Service in 1979 and his first operational tour was flying the Harrier GR3 in Germany. In 1988 and 1989 while based at Chivenor in North Devon, he was a Tactical Weapons Instructor on the British Aerospace Hawk, the RAF's advanced jet trainer, the aircraft flown by the Red Arrows. He also took time out to be the solo Hawk aerobatic display pilot. He won the prestigious Superkings Trophy for the best solo jet aerobatic display at the 1989 International Air Tattoo at Fairford, and he was awarded the Queen's Commendation for Valuable Service in the Air.

Simon first joined the Red Arrows for the 1991 season. In 1993, when he was Leader of the Synchro Pair, he was promoted to Squadron Leader, thereby finally establishing his credentials for a tour as Leader. However, one three-year tour with the Team drains a pilot, mentally and physically, and puts a considerable strain on family life. It would be demanding too much of any pilot to stay on as Red Leader immediately after completing a three-year stint with the Team. So, at the end of his three years,

Simon went off to Germany to fly Harriers again. A tour of duty on an operational front-line fast jet aircraft could by no stretch of the imagination be described as a 'rest', but at least it kept Simon out of the public eye for a while.

'What is the purpose of having the Red Arrows?' is another frequently asked question, usually posed by someone who begrudges the annual cost to the taxpayer. Until the end of the Cold War, the stock answer used to be 'recruitment' and it certainly was the case that many a young man and woman told the recruiting office staffs that they were inspired to apply for service in the RAF after watching a Red Arrows' display. Indeed, several of the current Red Arrows fall into that category. Perhaps the press-gangs of earlier centuries would not have been necessary had the Royal Navy been able to publicise its exploits by means of nationwide television and videos and if Captains of the Line had been required to make personal appearances at international regattas. There are no pressed men amongst the pilots; they are all volunteers.

Although the Cold War is over, promoting the RAF and thereby possibly assisting recruitment remains very important but the Red Arrows have found, or had thrust upon them, a new role – that of publicising what tends to be known as 'UK plc'. The highly successful tours of 1995 and 1996 across four continents were financed not by the tax-payer but from what the Team called 'our pot of gold', money provided by 16 British defence-related companies. The theme was 'Best of British', referring not just to the pilots and their skills but to the products of the companies that paid for the tours. There was ample evidence that the presence of the Red Arrows' pilots on trade stands at the international exhibitions

Following a tough but satisfying practice session, there's just time for a sandwich and coffee before debriefing. From left to right: Flight Lieutenant Andy Cubin, Flight Lieutenant Gary Waterfall (complete with mints), Squadron Leader Simon Meade and Flight Lieutenant Ian Smith, alias Reds 5, 3, 1 and 2 respectively.

attracted customers like bees to a honey pot. Whether or not that directly led to further orders is unclear, but the companies seemed to think that their sponsorship of the Red Arrows was money well spent. Certainly, orders for the latest version of the Hawk flooded in after the Red Arrows' tours. Would those companies do it again? There will be opportunities during Simon Meade's first year in command of the Team to put that question to the test.

Once selected, pilots, including Red Leader, expect to remain with the Team for a full three-year tour. In an ideal world the Team would consist of three first-year pilots, three in their second year and three in their final year, for in that way the greatest overall level of expertise would be maintained. However, the system is not fool-proof. One of the new 1990 pilots was replaced at the end of his first year; he went off to fly with what was then known as the Royal Flight and is now Number 32 (The Royal) Squadron. Had his successor stayed only two years the ideal rotation plan would have been maintained but, not surprisingly, he asked to remain for the full three years and was allowed to do so. Since then, there has been a four-two-three pattern of changes and the 'four year' includes a new leader. 1997 is one such year.

'For these first two weeks there will just be me and the three FNGs at work,' said Simon Meade to a visiting staff officer one morning, by way of explanation for the sparsely populated crew room. 'I need to get to know my new pilots and they have a lot of new procedures to learn before they can usefully start flying with the old hands. The five staying on from last season are still on their well-deserved leave.'

No one seems to know when the expression FNG was first used or by whom it was coined, but it has long been an indispensable part of the Red Arrows' somewhat quirky vocabulary. The NG part of the acronym stands for 'New Guy' and the initial F can be, and is, translated in a variety of ways. Pronounced quickly as a single word, effengee, it has become a very useful collective noun and there is no simpler nor more effective sobriquet to describe the new pilots in their first year. FNG appears in all manner of official correspondence from flying programmes to formal letters. In recent years, as is the way with these things, the idea has been adapted for wider use and so there is FNEng, referring to a new engineering officer, FNMange, for a new Team manager, and this year for the very first time FNB, referring to the new Boss, but it will be a brave man who refers to Simon Meade in that way to his face. In the spring of 1997 at RAF Akrotiri in Cyprus, when the pilots short-listed for selection for the 1998 Team spend a week with the Team, they will be known simply as FFNGs, the additional F being completely untranslatable but instantly understood.

FNGs have to know their place in the scheme of things. They are the juniors and, like all juniors, they will be exposed to much banter and ribbing. They will enjoy their first two weeks but will look forward with a certain degree of trepidation to week three.

A New Beginning

'My father was a flying instructor, based here at Cranwell among other places, and so I was exposed to flying from a very early age,' announced Flight Lieutenant Ian Smith, one of the FNGs. His youthful looks and ready smile belie his 32 years. He was born in the RAF Hospital at Nocton Hall, just ten miles to the north of Cranwell. Now 6ft 3in tall and broad-shouldered, he has quite a squeeze to fit his frame into a Hawk cockpit. 'In my first tour I flew the giant Chinook helicopter on 18 Squadron in Germany, but later I converted onto Jaguars – much more exciting. I applied to join the Red Arrows as soon as I had the necessary qualifications and I was fortunate to be selected the first time.'

Ian, who is single, is very keen on sports and is even taking up golf, almost a prerequisite for being a member of the Red Arrows. He has a special interest in motor bikes and sports cars and, if he cannot get enough aerobatic flying with the Red Arrows, he can take to the air in his own aeroplane, a Christen Eagle fully aerobatic biplane which he keeps in a corner of one of the Red Arrows' hangars. A now little-used regulation, dating back to the RAF's earliest years, allows pilots to keep their own personal aircraft in RAF hangars when space is available. Smithy will have to learn to get used to repartee from his colleagues about his 'humble' beginnings on helicopters, but before the winter is out he will have become something of a national hero.

Flight Lieutenant Gary Waterfall, not quite 30 years of age, the same height as Ian but very slim, also just fits into the cockpit. He, too, was born in an RAF Hospital,

It is largely during the winter months that all the heavy duty maintenance is done on the Team's jets, including the application of a fresh coat of paint.

The Red Arrows have been thrilling audiences worldwide since the establishment of the Team in 1965.

at Wegberg in Germany, where his father was serving as a Warrant Officer engineer. Gary was educated at Kings School, Grantham, just down the road from Cranwell, where he was a member of that school's Combined Cadet Force. 'I always wanted to join the RAF,' said Gary and he did so at the age of 18 in September 1985. Gary is one of four former Harrier pilots in the 1997 Team. Before joining the Red Arrows he was the RAF's solo Harrier display pilot and he flew 64 displays in Europe.

'Being selected to join the Red Arrows is the fulfil-ment of a life-long ambition,' said Gary. He would with-draw early from the Team's Cyprus detachment in spring 1997 to fly home to England on a British Airways' flight, leaving a spare pilot to fly his Hawk back to Cranwell, and shortly after that he was to have have an embarrass-ing accident that would keep him off flying altogether for several weeks.

At 34, the third new pilot, Flight Lieutenant Andy Cubin, is the oldest FNG for many years, a fact which leads to ribbing from his team mates from time to time. Andy always has a grin on his face and nothing seems to faze him. He is a very experienced pilot with three con-secutive tours and more than 3,000 flying hours on Jaguar aircraft under his belt. During that time he was the

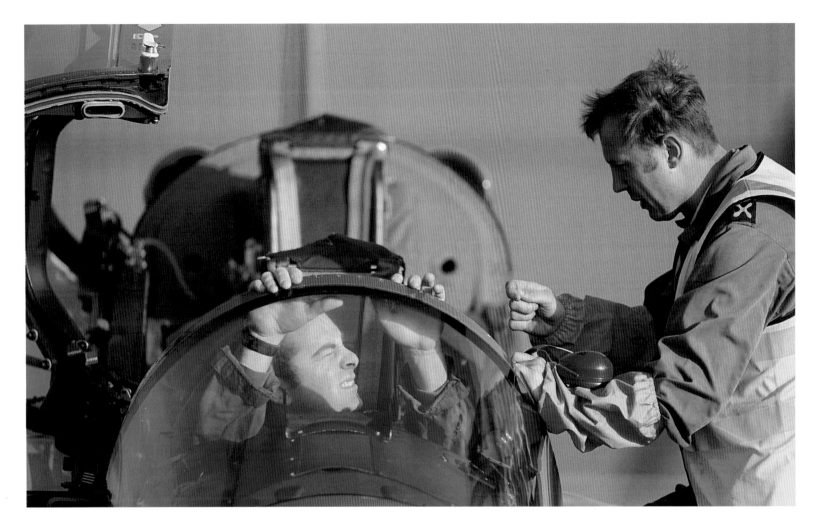

RAF's solo Jaguar display pilot, logging performances at over 150 displays.

'Dad was a Meteorological Officer,' says Andy. 'He worked on many different airfields and so we moved around quite a lot. There's no place I can really call my home town. Although I was educated at Stowmarket High School in Suffolk, I was actually born in the Shetland Islands at Lerwick. Dad took me to see an air show at Turnhouse Airport near Edinburgh in 1971 – when I was a very young lad. The Red Arrows were performing there and I thought "That's for me!" And here I am.' And soon after Christmas 1996 Andy was to take a day off to be presented to the Queen at Buckingham Palace.

At last, while the five pilots staying on from the last

The ground crew really are the unsung heroes of the Red Arrows. It is their responsibility to ensure the Team's Hawks are serviceable with all systems functioning properly. The pilots' lives depend on their professionalism.

Team were still enjoying their end of season leave, the day of reckoning arrived for the three new pilots. The many weeks of waiting since their selection, back in spring 1996, were over. Whatever they had done in the past, however experienced they were in their previous role and whatever their seniority, they were now the FNGs.

Day one is for flying check rides with the new

(Left) An asymmetrical six-ship formation loop in the clear deep blue October sky overhead Cranwell. Now the new pilots are up to speed, they are joined by the second and third year 'old hands'.

(Above) Having landed, the same six jets taxi in towards their hard stands. Throughout the winter months the Team will fly three practice sorties each day, the formation gradually building its repertoire of manoeuvres. Sometimes the number of jets flying will depend upon the number available due to maintenance commitments.

Squadron Commander. Almost without exception, pilots hate flying tests – and the new pilots were no exceptions. No matter how skilful you are, and no one doubted the FNGs' professional skills, tests can easily go wrong through no fault of your own. When that happens, it is known euphemistically as 'having a bad day'. All three of the new pilots had flown the Hawk earlier in their careers, but none was in current flying practice on the aircraft when he joined the Team. Simon and the new pilots had spent a few days at the RAF's Advanced Flying Training School at Valley on the island of Anglesey, refreshing their basic techniques and practising emergencies and other procedures in the flight simulator.

'I'm responsible for everything that happens on the Squadron,' explained Simon Meade, in the quiet yet authoritative tone to which the members of his Squadron would soon become accustomed. He knows that it is essential for any new commander to establish his authority as quickly as possible, especially when there are others of equal rank under command. In the case of the world's premier aerobatic team there have, in years gone by, been those of higher rank than the Leader who sought to exert undue influence in the day-to-day running of the Squadron. In no position of authority does the old adage 'With the glory goes the responsibility' have more validity than in the office of the Leader of the Red Arrows.

'As far as the pilots are concerned,' continued Simon, 'I have all their confidential flying reports from earlier tours, but the only way I can satisfy myself that they're up to scratch and meet the high professional standards required of them is to fly with each of them in turn. That's the aim of the Squadron Commander's check ride – it's the same on all flying squadrons, not just the Reds.'

Every active RAF pilot has a number of other check rides each year; rank and seniority does not debar them, nor does experience. There are two main tests: an annual Instrument Rating Test, usually flown with the Squadron's own examiner, and a periodic handling check flown with the Trappers – the widely used nickname for the Examiners of the Central Flying School.

The Red Arrows' Instrument Rating Examiner is Flight Lieutenant Sean Perrett, a former Harrier pilot and Hawk instructor just starting his third and final year with the Team. His Grandfather was a pilot with the Royal Naval Air Service during the First World War and his Father was a National Service pilot with the Army, so flying is in his blood. During the Far East tour of December 1995, Sean was badly injured in a road accident on the island of Langkawi in Malaysia when a car carrying three of the pilots was struck by a lorry at a road junction. Sean was flown back to England to have his broken shoulder pinned and, to his dismay, took no part in the tours of Australia and Singapore in early 1996. One consolation was that he was able to be present at the birth of his second son, Corey. He was fully recovered in time for the 1996 European display season.

Even Sean has to undergo the instrument flying test, with an independent examiner from the CFS Examining Wing, and in his case it would be extremely embarrassing were he to fail. He came in from leave to renew his own ticket and explained the format of a typical test.

'The sortie lasts about an hour. The pilot under test flies entirely by reference to instruments and without looking out of the cockpit. When I'm the examiner, I fly in the rear cockpit. I have to satisfy myself that the pilot is safe to fly his aircraft in cloud and to land it when the cloud base is as low as 200 feet above the ground or when the horizontal visibility is barely half a nautical mile.'

To ensure that the pilots can operate in accordance with civilian procedures in international airways, as they do on almost every flight outside UK airspace, the test includes at least one airways sector flying in among the airliners. The pilot under test has to do all his own navigation and radio calls, as well as fly the aircraft to a high degree of accuracy. There is a very high work load, not helped by the lack of modern avionics in the 15-year-old Hawks flown by the Red Arrows.

'Sometime during the flight there will be some recoveries from unusual positions (UPs),' continued Sean, warming to his theme. 'I generate the UPs by carrying out a number of high g rolling and pitching manoeuvres while the other pilot keeps his eyes firmly inside the cockpit.'

UPs simulate disorientation in cloud, one of the most frightening and dangerous things that can happen to any pilot. The object is to regain straight and level flight with minimum loss of height without looking out at the real world. 'Flying by the seat of your pants', a technique oft recommended by pilots in past eras, has no relevance in modern flying – if it ever had. The seat of the pants can give very misleading indications when you cannot see the real horizon; only the flight instruments can be trusted.

'Student pilots sometimes think it helps to cheat by trying to look out of the cockpit at the horizon without

The winter training period is always a balancing act. The Team need to practice regularly, gradually progressing towards the psychological achievement of the first nine-ship, usually around December or early January. Frustratingly, however, maintenance and the good old Lincolnshire weather can delay matters.

the examiner noticing,' continued Sean. 'They're very wrong! Experienced pilots know that it is absolutely essential for their own safety and confidence to practice UPs properly.'

The recovery to base at the end of the high altitude

work will be a very demanding high-speed descent using stand-by attitude instruments, not the easiest of instruments to interpret. Once at low level, the pilot has to fly a number of airfield approaches entirely on instruments down to Decision Height, the height at which he must overshoot and climb away to safety if the ground or the runway is not sighted.

'We all used our instrument ratings to maximum effect on the way to South Africa last year,' said Sean. 'Approaching Nairobi International Airport, we descended through thick frontal cloud from 40,000 feet and only came out at 400 feet, just above decision height. Not something I'd care to repeat in a hurry.'

The results of the Squadron Commander's check are known only to Simon and the pilot concerned, but it can be safely assumed that all three FNGs reached the required standard because later that same afternoon, the afternoon of day one, they flew their first four-ship formation sortie in relative privacy overhead Scampton airfield, the Red Arrows' former home until earlier in the year, 20 miles to the north of Cranwell.

The FNGs had flown formation many times before as a normal routine on their operational squadrons, but their first sortie with the Red Arrows was different. Each was anxious not to make a fool of himself, especially as all Red Arrows' flights with two or more aircraft are recorded on video for use at post-flight debriefings. What the FNGs had not realised was that two 1996 pilots who had just left the Team, John Rands and Spike Jepson, both still living in married quarters at RAF Scampton, were outside watching their first formation attempts. This led to an unofficial debriefing and a little banter a short while later. It could never be said that the Red Arrows' pilots are shy of criticising each other's efforts!

A member of the ground crew prepares to stow his Mae West as Cubes sorts out his helmet and oxygen mask so that it's all set for the next sortie.

Returning jets kick up droplets of water off the shower-soaked taxiway as they roll back in.

After the stress of the Squadron Commander's check ride and the first formation sortie, the FNGs were raring to go, but the Tuesday of the first week dawned misty and raining. The forecast for the whole of eastern England was very poor. Not wishing to waste a single day, Red Leader decided to fly with the other three over to Anglesey where the weather was clear and sunny. That day two four-aircraft formation sorties

were flown over the relief landing ground at Mona, close to Valley and well away from the prying eyes of Rands and Jepson. As the weather at Cranwell remained below landing limits all day, the four pilots stayed overnight at Valley. Thus they missed the opportunity of meeting Sir Harry Secombe who came to Cranwell to film an interview for the BBC television programme *Songs of Praise*.

'I see the Red Arrows have flown off. I suppose they heard I was coming!' quipped Sir Harry with his inimitable chuckle. The BBC producer wanted to take advantage of the ratings appeal of the Red Arrows and so he used the remaining red Hawk aircraft as a backdrop for an interview with England Rugby star Flight Lieutenant Rory Underwood, the rather tenuous link being that Rory, now stationed at Cranwell, had recently completed a tour of duty on Hawk aircraft.

On day four the weather was much improved. Two more four-aircraft sorties were flown at Mona before the pilots returned to base. The following day, Her Majesty the Queen visited Lincoln to open the new University of Lincolnshire and Humberside. The pilots had to stay well clear of Lincoln, but if the Royal Visit had been only one month earlier the full team would doubtless have been invited to make a Royal flypast. As it was, someone put out a false story that the Red Arrows would be flying over the new University campus to salute the Queen.

The brief Indian summer continued and by the end of week two the four pilots had flown 29 sorties each. One of them, however, was not entirely happy.

'I've an aching back,' complained Andy Cubin rue-fully. 'I can't find a really comfortable position in the air-craft. If I put my ejection seat low enough to see through one part of the canopy, my knees would smash against the cockpit coaming if I had to eject. If I put the ejection seat higher so that I can see clearly through another panel, my head would get jammed against the cockpit canopy and I'd probably break my neck if I had to eject. I don't like either of those options, so I've put my ejection seat in a middling position and that means I have to twist my neck awkwardly to see the Leader. I expect I'll get used to it,' he added with a grin.

With that, the new pilots' honeymoon period was over. After the weekend the other five pilots would return from leave and the winter training programme would move into top gear. For the very first time the flying units at Cranwell and nearby stations would have to get used to Red Arrows' winter operations – and so would the inhabitants of nearby villages. Cranwell would never be the same again.

Following each practice flight, both the jets' fuel tanks and smoke pods need to be replenished in readiness for the next. Steve Gardner ensures the correct quantity of white smoke-producing diesel is pumped into the streamlined pod slung beneath the Hawk's belly.

A Matter of Side

'The two positions nearest to the Leader are generally reckoned to be the easiest to fly,' explained Simon Meade in the Squadron Briefing Room, juggling ten two-dimensional model Hawk aircraft on a magnetic board. There is one numbered model representing each of the nine display pilots and one for Red 10, the Team Manager.

It has long been a convention in the Royal Air Force that formation positions to the right of the leader are given an even number and those to the left an odd number. In the basic Diamond Nine formation, the Synchro Pair, Reds 6 and 7, fly directly line astern of the Leader. Within the Red Arrows, position numbers are used not only on the radio in the air, but also for all manner of written and verbal communications on the ground. Unless he becomes a member of the Synchro Pair, each pilot can expect to spend all three years flying on the side of the formation on which he started.

'I've put Ian Smith in the 2 slot on my right, and Gary Waterfall in the 3 slot on my left,' continued Simon. 'So that means Smithy can expect to stay on the right-hand side, moving out one place to Red 4 in his second year and then one position rearwards to Red 8 in his third and final year. Similarly, Gary can expect to move to Red 5 and 9 in his later years. The third new pilot, Andy Cubin, goes into the 5 slot on the left-hand side – two aircraft out from me. One of those three will be selected for the Synchro Pair next year. Synchro Leader gets to choose his own number two – subject to my approval of course.'

Being a left- or a right-hand side man is important. The pilots spend much of their time in the air looking out to one particular side of the cockpit towards the Leader, so their neck muscles get used to being cranked over to that side. Experience over many years has shown that a former Red 2 flies better and is more comfortable in later years as Red 4 and Red 8 than if he were to move to the other side of the formation. The same principle applies to Reds 3, 5 and 9.

'The further away you are from the Leader, the more difficult it is to maintain an accurate position,' explained Richie Matthews, the Squadron Executive Officer, Red Leader's right-hand man in both senses of the phrase. In his teens, Richie was an accomplished cricketer and in one school match he took all the opposition wickets. 'Sadly, they were playing a man short so I was denied the magic 10-wicket innings,' he recalls. 'Too much sport can be counter-productive. Divided loyalty between cricket and schoolwork meant that I was lucky to gain entry into the RAF because my exam results reflected too many overs bowled!'

Like many RAF pilots, Richie's route into the Service was via the Air Training Corps in his home town, Ashford in Kent. He reached the rank of Flight Sergeant in the ATC and later was awarded an RAF Flying Scholarship which gave him 30 hours of flying with a civilian flying club at the RAF's expense. His first operational tour was flying Jaguars with No 41(F) Squadron at Coltishall in Norfolk. Richie is in his third and final year with the Team and now flies as Red 8. The coming winter months would be both painful and frustrating for him.

'Reds 4 and 5 have to try and smooth out any inaccuracies introduced by 2 and 3,' continued Richie. 'They do that by trying to look through the nearest aircraft and watching the Leader. Of course, you can't completely ignore the aircraft nearest to you. If Red 4 was to try and follow every movement of Red 2 quite a whip could develop and that would be very off-putting for me at the back in the 8 slot. The raggedness would show to the people on the ground.'

In the horizontal plane there are two reference

points on the nearest aircraft for each formation shape; one gives the correct fore and aft position and the other gives the correct distance out from the adjacent aircraft. If both references are maintained accurately, by use of the throttle, ailerons and occasionally the rudder, the principles of geometry ensure that the aircraft are in the right position. The position of the aircraft relative to each other in the vertical plane, controlled by the elevator, also varies according to the formation shape being flown. The FNGs are taught what references to look for but eventually they pick out points which work best for them.

Flight Lieutenant Tim 'Timmy' Couston, one of the Synchro Pair – the duo that perform the dramatic head-to-head passes – loads up to eight times the force of gravity (g) as he executes a maximum rate turn, wing tip vortices mixing with the jet's smoke in the moist air.

An indication of how important the formation reference points are can be seen on borrowed aircraft used at times during the winter. Because the paint scheme on borrowed aircraft is different from that on the Red Arrows' own aircraft, the formation reference

Tim Couston and Dave Stobie, alias the Synchro Pair, perfect their daring duet above Cranwell. It's not really that close – it's just an illusion, or 'fudge' as they call it.

points have to be painted on the loan aircraft. When the Red Arrows flew with a British Airways Concorde for a joint flypast in celebration of Heathrow Airport's 50th birthday in 1996, formation reference points were indicated by red spots specially painted above one of the passengers' windows on each side of the Concorde airframe.

As recently as 1989, first-year pilots were often relegated to the back of the formation. In fact, of the 102 pilots that had displayed in public with the Team up to the end of the 1996 season, 18 started their tour as Red 8 and 22 started out as Red 9. The rationale was that if you made a mistake 'down the back' it had little effect on the other pilots, but the public could see who was to blame if the formation was not perfect. Another theory, reinforcing the first, said that it was better to put the most experienced pilots in the 2 and 3 positions to give the whole formation a very steady foundation. In recent years, however, the rear four aircraft, Reds 6, 7, 8 and 9, have been flying ever more demanding manoeuvres in the second half of the show. It is now considered better

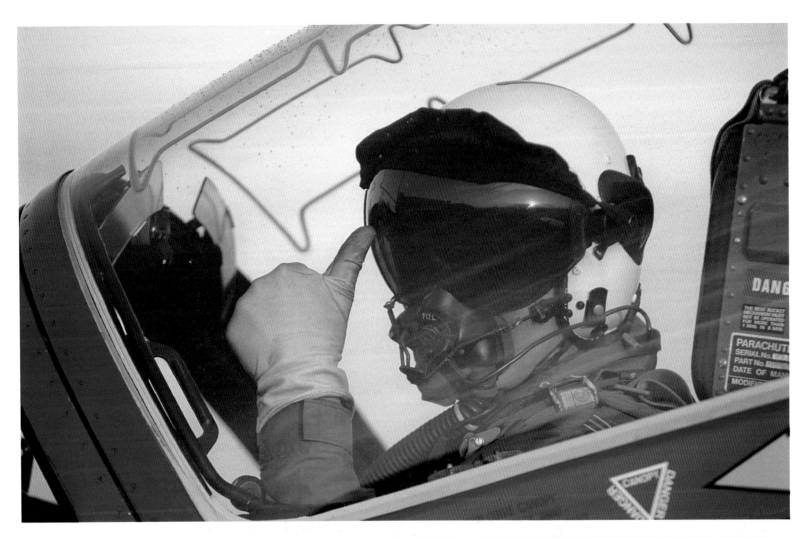

Red 2, Flight Lieutenant Ian Smith, is ready to roll. Built in to the canopy above Smithy's head is the Miniature Detonating Cord (MDC). Should he be forced to eject, the MDC would explode, shattering the canopy and thus providing the void through which he and the seat would be projected.

for those positions to be filled by the most experienced pilots.

Andy Offer, who had been Red 2 in 1996, moved out one place to Red 4 for 1997. Andy hails from Bishops Stortford and was educated at St Edmunds College in Ware, where he was a member of the Combined Cadet

*Celebrations are afoot in the Red Arrows' crew room for Gary Waterfall's
30th birthday. Smithy marks this auspicious occasion with a splendid
little chocolate cake, complete with necessary pyrotechnics.*

Force. He is no stranger to display flying. He started his
operational flying career as a flying instructor and was
the Jet Provost solo display pilot before moving on to the
front line and converting to Harriers. In 1995 he was the
solo Harrier display pilot and performed his thrilling
routine at 48 public displays, the last one just a few days

before joining the Red Arrows. Still only 30 years old, he
was promoted to Squadron Leader on 1 July 1996.

'There's no problem my being a Squadron Leader on
the Team with a Squadron Leader Boss,' said Andy. 'I'm
not the only one, anyway, because the Manager is always
a Squadron Leader. In the past there have often been
Squadron Leaders on the Team. We're nine headstrong
blokes; you get respect on the Team for the way you fly,
not the rank you hold. The only difference the rank
makes in this job is that I get paid more than the rest!'

Dave Stobie, or Stobes as he is known to all his

friends, joined the Team at the same time as Andy Offer in late-1995. Stobes was born in Germany where his father was working as a civil servant for the British government.

'I first saw the Red Arrows in the late 70s at RAF Bruggen and I decided then that I wanted to be a pilot, although I don't think I aspired to joining the Team at that early stage.'

David, who is easily recognised by his distinguished looking, shiny forehead, has been both instructor and examiner on Hawk aircraft. In 1994 he was the Hawk solo display pilot. Following Sean Perrett's injury in Malaysia, Stobes took over the 3 slot for the first half of the displays during the rest of the tours of the Far East and Australia. He fitted in so skilfully that most spectators never realised they were watching an understudy. The second halves were flown with just eight aircraft because there simply was not enough time for him to practice the complicated, high energy manoeuvres. Thus Stobes became the first pilot in the history of the Red Arrows to display in a green flying suit. Dave flew as Red 3 in his own right with the 1996 Team and at the end of the season was selected by 1997 Synchro Leader Tim Couston to be Synchro 2 for the year.

Another six-footer, Flight Lieutenant Tim Couston is something of a rarity among Red Arrows – a former Buccaneer pilot. He flew 14 combat missions during the Gulf War and yet still found time to be the solo Buccaneer display pilot and take part in deployments to Bermuda. He joined the Red Arrows in the autumn of 1994 at the end of a tour of duty as a Hawk weapons instructor.

'This business of side is not quite so straightforward for me. I started out as a right-hand side man, in the 4 slot. In my second year, as Synchro 2, I spent the first half of every show in the 7 slot on the centre-line at the back of the formation, or out on the left-hand side in formations such as Big Nine and Big Vixen. Now I'm right in the middle of the Diamond Nine or out to the right, behind Red 2 and 4, looking to the left again.'

The Team's Uncle

'The winter flying programme is based around slots,' explained Richie Matthews, one of whose jobs as the Squadron Executive Officer is to write the daily flying programme. 'A slot is a 30-minute period in which the Reds have complete freedom of movement. Other aircraft cannot take off and land while we are practising overhead so they have to fit their programme around ours. In the early part of the winter we need six slots almost every day – three slots for the Synchro pair to practice on their own, inter-spaced with three slots for the rest of the formation. It was quite straightforward while we were based at Scampton but it's a bit more complicated now we're at Cranwell because the Commandant and the Wing Commander have to supervise some of our early sorties from the ground.'

The Red Arrows had moved to Cranwell from Scampton during the 1995 winter tour to the Far East. Cranwell is a very active flying training airfield in its own right and it is surrounded by other busy RAF flying bases. Eight miles to the north is Waddington, home of two squadrons of E3 Sentry airborne early warning aircraft and a squadron of Nimrod reconnaissance aircraft and which often has visiting fighters from European air forces. Coningsby, a Tornado base, is only 12 miles to the east of Cranwell. The climb out and descent lanes for Coningsby's aircraft pass close to Cranwell's overhead and impose severe restrictions on aircraft flying in the Cranwell circuit in some weather conditions. Just five miles south of Cranwell is the very busy Barkston Heath airfield from where the RAF's Joint Elementary Flying Training School operates.

The Cranwell circuit and surrounding area is too busy to accommodate Red Arrows' practices six times a day in the winter months. The Team needs a large volume of airspace guaranteed to be free of all other aircraft in which to practice. For many years the airspace above the runway at Scampton, officially known as Restricted Area R313, has been reserved for the exclusive use of the Team. All military and civilian pilots know that they cannot enter R313 without specific permission to do so. The area stretches out five nautical miles from the centre of the airfield and extends from ground level up to 9,500 feet above the ground. Even though Scampton station closed down at the end of 1995, R313 was retained and the Red Arrows continue to carry out most of their practice flying overhead Scampton. Simon Meade's first months in command was the first winter this arrangement had been put into operation.

'There's a one-way system with a clockwise flow for all low flying aircraft in the congested Lincoln area,' explained Corporal Tim Smith, the Air Traffic Control Assistant who, together with Senior Aircraftman Andy Foxhall, runs the Red Arrows' own flight planning cell on the upper floor next to the briefing room. 'When the Reds depart from Cranwell for a practice at Scampton, they skirt around the west of Lincoln City. They remain at low level to pass underneath any aircraft flying in the Waddington circuit. It takes them three minutes to fly the 20 miles from Cranwell to Scampton. On the southbound leg from Scampton back to Cranwell, the Reds keep to the east of the City.'

Although the one-way system is specifically designed to reduce the risk of low level conflictions, it also has the beneficial effect of decreasing by half the noise nuisance for those villagers who do not appreciate the Red Arrows passing overhead several times a day. The southbound leg passes very close to WAVE, the RAF Waddington Aircraft Viewing Enclosure, a recently constructed haven off to one side of the very busy A15, which has a splendid panoramic view over Waddington airfield. Looking towards the north on a clear day, with the magnificent Lincoln Cathedral standing out against the skyline on top of Lindum Hill, aviation enthusiasts logging aircraft movements in and out of Waddington have a spectacular long distance view of the Red Arrows'

red, white and blue smoke trails as the aircraft loop and roll over Scampton, five miles north of the city. They can then follow the aircrafts' progress as they transit around Lincoln, close to WAVE, and back towards Cranwell.

When the Red Arrows practice overhead Scampton airfield, Air Traffic Control is manned and the emergency services are on immediate readiness. Although landings by the whole Team at Scampton are not routinely planned, the 9,000-foot runway is maintained in a serviceable condition and is immediately available in any emergency. This facility would be used several times during the winter of 1996-7. There is also a one-man bird-scaring unit manned by a civilian. His primary job is to drive around the airfield before the Hawks arrive and attempt to clear off any concentrations of birds. For as long as the Team is practising overhead, he keeps watch and can warn the air traffic controller of any new bird concentrations that might pose a hazard to the aircraft. When an aircraft is travelling at 400 miles an hour, a collision with a bird can have a devastating effect – as one of the pilots was to discover for himself before the end of the winter training season.

The bird scarer has to be able to recognise the species of the birds flying over the airfield. He has a selection of tapes of birds' distress calls which he can play over loudspeakers, thereby encouraging the birds to disperse. Some of the birds, however, have got used to this ploy and tend to ignore the distress calls unless the operator also gives chase in his Land Rover. Other birds, presumably those that live permanently on Scampton airfield, have grown used to both the bird scarer and to the Red Arrows' Hawks. These birds can often be seen apparently mimicking the Reds, doing their own formation aerobatics just above grass level while the mechani-

When not in use, the Red Arrows' Hawks are kept undercover in two hangars at Cranwell, the roof over their heads helping to preserve the immaculate shine on the paintwork.

(Previous page) The long runway at RAF Akrotiri recedes into the background as Red Leader loops his Hawk, the remaining six jets fanning out to the left and right in the Vertical Split.

(Right) Each April, the Red Arrows deploy to RAF Akrotiri in Cyprus, taking advantage of the generally favourable weather to be found there, permitting three uninterrupted sorties per day to perfect their display.

cal Hawks are performing two or three hundred feet above them. It seems that birds cannot loop the loop, but they certainly can perform steep turns and wing-overs in perfect formation.

Every practice by two or more aircraft and every public display is recorded on video. One of the Red Arrows' ground crew travels by road from Cranwell every flying day to operate the camera to cover the Scampton operations. Eventually there will be a high definition video link between Scampton and Cranwell which will allow the video man in front of Air Traffic Control at Scampton to send live pictures to a VCR in the Team's briefing room at Cranwell. There either Tim or Andy will record the pictures, so providing the Team Leader with the evidence he needs for the post-flight debriefings. The videos can also be used if there is any dispute about the height at which the aircraft were flying or if there is an accident. Until the video link has been established, one of the Hawks has to land on the runway at Scampton at the end of each session, pick up the cassette from the cameraman and then roar off to catch up with the other aircraft.

People often ask what the pilots' wives think about the job. Aimée Perrett's answer is fairly typical: 'I don't really worry about the flying. Sean has always wanted to do this and I know that all the pilots trust each other. I think we all get used to the flying – it's their job after all – but the routine is more difficult to get used to. In many ways the lifestyle is better than it is on a front line squadron – at least it is in the winter months when they

The nine-ship Red Arrows formation loop in characteristically perfect Diamond Nine. For optimum 'shape' this formation must be viewed from Display Datum – the central axis on which the display is orientated. The slight imbalance we see here is due to the fact that we are viewing the formation from one side, not centrally.

come home most evenings. Front line aircrew spend a lot of time away from home these days – and that's all the year round not just in the summer months. The real problem with the Red Arrows' summer programme is that it's so unpredictable. Children can get used to Daddy being away for weeks on end, as they are on operational squadrons, but the Red Arrows sometimes go away for just one night and sometimes for longer; it's really confusing for young children.

'I never worried about Sean until he had his acci-

For the second half of the 20-minute display, Reds 1 to 5, collectively known as Enid, separate from Gypo, Reds 6 to 9, the rear four which includes the Synchro Pair, in the Four/Five Split.

dent in Langkawi just before last Christmas. Of course, that was a road accident and had nothing to do with flying, but if the Team has to go back to Langkawi at the end of 1997, I know I'll worry about him then. The wives do quite a lot of things together when the husbands are

A bird's-eye view of Reds 1 to 5, plus 8 and 9, as they perform the Vertical Split. Moments later, the Synchro Pair, Reds 6 and 7, will run in from crowd left and right for their Opposition Loop.

away. That's simply because several of us live quite close to each other. We also compare notes about what's going on at the Squadron. Sometimes, when they are at home, we have to trawl through their briefcases to find out where they're going next. I think they're so tired when they get home that they simply don't want to start talking about the job and so we never know what's going on.'

Close supervision does not end at Simon Meade. The Red Arrows have their own set of standard operating procedures (SOPs), approved and signed by a two-star Air Marshal at Command Headquarters. The SOPs aim to cover both routine and non-routine eventualities. They are amended from time to time to reflect changing circumstances and they are consulted frequently to confirm who is authorised to do what and when. On a day-to-day basis, higher level supervision of the Team is vested in Wing Commander Dick Johnston. His official title is Wing Commander RAFAT, but within the Squadron he is usually known just as 'the Wing Commander', except, that is, by Andy Offer who always refers to Dick by the quaintly old-fashioned expression 'Wingco'. Although Wing Commander Johnston has an office in the Team's HQ, he is a senior staff officer working directly for the Commandant of the Central Flying School and Dick is always at pains to point out to visitors that he does not command the Red Arrows.

'Supervision of the Team's flying is a straightforward aspect of my job,' explained Wing Commander Johnston. 'Although I've never been a Red Arrow, I can utilise my 25-years' flying experience – much of it spent flying and instructing on the Hawk – together with judgement and common sense, to cast an impartial eye over the Team's flying activities both in training and on the display circuit. The other half of my job is far less easy to define. My predecessor described the job to me as "a bit like being the Team's Uncle". I range from being the sounding board on which the guys vent their frustrations, to being the front-man for negotiating on the Team's behalf with the higher command echelons. One of my primary functions,

I believe, is to keep the burden of staff work off Simon's shoulders to allow him to concentrate on his primary task of leading the Team in the air.'

In order to do his job, Wing Commander RAFAT is required to fly regularly with Team members – and he needs no encouragement to do so. He also frequently watches the practices from the ground, which is fine during the summer but less enjoyable standing in the rain on an icy, wind-swept airfield in mid-winter. Whenever there is an air test that needs to be flown after an aircraft has been serviced, or when a pilot has, perhaps, reported some unusual handling characteristic, Wing Commander Johnston is always at the front of the

Viewed from on high, the colourful Red Arrows create a wonderful picture, contrasting dramatically with the deep blue of the Mediterranean.

queue and never seems too busy to leave his desk and take to the air. He often flies a spare Hawk on Team detachments, especially on overseas trips when 11 aircraft are needed, and uses the radio callsign Red 11.

Before his first year in the job is over, Dick will need to bring all his flying skills and experience into play when he has to make an unscheduled diversion, short of fuel and in appalling weather conditions, to an airfield near his home in South Wales.

SOPs

'Every Red Arrows' sortie, practice or display is preceded by a formal briefing which typically lasts about 15 minutes,' said Squadron Leader Meade. 'It's something of a ritual, but it's vitally important. It doesn't matter how many times we fly, we always go through the sortie in detail to make absolutely certain that everyone knows exactly what is planned. If we have a television crew recording the briefing, as we often do, no interruptions are allowed – no re-takes. If they miss something at the briefing, that's it, unless they can come back on another occasion. We often let our visitors sit in at the briefings but we don't permit them to interrupt with questions either.'

A large number of companies lend 'support' to the Team in a variety of ways. By way of thanks, those companies are invited to visit the Team during the winter

A pilot's-eye view from Red 5, Andy Cubin's jet, as Enid follow my leader down in Caterpillar formation. The extended slabs visible beneath the rear fuselage of Reds 2, 3 and 4 are the jets' airbrakes.

training period. Sometimes the companies use their visit as an opportunity to entertain clients of their own. The corporate visitors are, naturally, disappointed that they usually have no opportunity to watch the main formation working up, but at least they can watch them take off and land.

Corporate visitors are scheduled to visit on virtually every working day during the winter. Visiting groups are limited to nine at a time so that they can be hosted on a one-to-one basis. The FNGs will find that there is very little privacy at the Red Arrows and they will have to get accustomed to the fact that there will be hundreds of visitors during the winter. However tired they may be, however often they are asked the same question, the pilots –

and the ground crew – must always bear in mind the importance of being polite to visitors.

Everything operational is governed by procedures. 'This will be an SOP sortie', means that the flight will be conducted in accordance with the standard operating procedures. Pre-flight briefings start at the appointed time to the nearest second. A one-minute warning bell is

It is only when one actually flies with the Red Arrows in the formation that one appreciates just how close they are, how much relative movement there is as each jet kicks and bucks in its own air space and how hard the pilots have to work, continuously correcting with air frame controls and power.

An exterior view of Caterpillar,
as Reds 1 to 5 arc down with
airbrakes extended.

rung – Gary Waterfall has the onerous task of sounding it. Woe betide anyone who is late and woe betide Gary if he forgets to ring the bell. The Team Leader then gives a five second countdown from the radio-controlled clock on the wall so that all the pilots may synchronise their watches. Simon conducts the briefing standing on a low dais in front of the magnetic board. At some stage he will suddenly pose a series of 'what if' questions for the pilots to deal with.

'You have an engine problem and have to abort take off at 100 knots. Red 2 what would you do?'

'Red 4 you lose sight of Red 2 on the re-join. What do you do?'

'Red 5 your engine surges at the top of a loop. What are your actions?'

The flight line where the aircraft are parked is about 300 metres from the Squadron HQ. Sometimes the pilots walk out, but usually they travel together in a self-drive minibus. The ground crew will already have set all the cockpit switches in the correct position so the pilots do not have to carry out many of the pre-starting checks themselves. That is SOP. This procedure takes some getting used to because it is unlike normal RAF squadron practice, but it saves a lot of time. It also means the pilots must have complete confidence in their 'techies'. Once an aircraft has been 'prepped' for flight, no one else is allowed into the cockpit. If, for some reason, someone does go into the cockpit, then all the pre-flight checks have to be done again, just in case a switch or lever has been moved.

Each pilot is on his own until the order to start engines is given by the Leader and thereafter everything is done as a team, by the clock. When everyone is ready, Red Leader will call for taxi clearance from Air Traffic Control. As each aircraft moves forward from its parking slot, the pilot checks that the wheel brakes are functioning normally and then all the aircraft move into close formation to taxi out to the runway. They taxi alternately to the left and right of the taxiway to avoid being directly in line with the jet wash from the preceding aircraft.

In the air, the pilots have more to do than simply flying the aircraft. For a start, they have to memorise the sequence of display manoeuvres; it is not a case of 'follow my leader' because if they did that they would always be behind the action. All the pilots have to act instantly on the Leader's executive word of command. The Leader calls most manoeuvres before initiating them: 'Diamond go'; 'pulling up'; 'tightening'; 'throttling back'; 'air brakes, air brakes, go'; 'breaking, breaking, go'; and so on. The pilots must know which is the executive word or syllable of command. Simon's intonation and cadence are all important, particularly as far as last year's pilots are concerned. They had got used to the way John Rands gave commands; Simon gives them as he remembers them from his last tour and has adapted them for his own style. The FNGs have to learn the system; last year's pilots have to forget the old system and learn the new.

Very closely allied to the sequence of the aerobatics is the question of escape manoeuvres – and this is very much an individual problem. If a pilot falls out of position within the formation, or if he has an emergency which necessitates leaving the formation quickly, there are five possible ways he could go: pulling up or pushing down, breaking left or right, or decelerating and 'dropping off the back'. Pushing and pulling describes what the pilot does to the control column, not what the resultant effect is. For example, if the pilot pushes the control column forward when the aircraft is inverted at the top of a loop, the aircraft will bunt and climb. This might be the only safe escape route for the Leader. Red 6, in the middle of the Diamond Nine, has the most constraints. He cannot move left or right and he cannot afford to decelerate because Red 7 is right behind him, but he still has the options of pushing or pulling. Depending on the circumstances and the aircraft's attitude, there will generally be only one safe escape route. Any pilot who departs from the formation must tell the Leader in case he has not seen the incident in his rear-view mirror. Simon then has to decide whether to continue with the manoeuvre or roll out to straight and level flight to sort things out.

It is imperative that the pilots know instinctively what their immediate actions are in the event of emergencies. Quite a dramatic problem, an engine surge, can arise when a pilot inadvertently allows his aircraft to rise up directly behind another's jet pipe. When this happens, the very hot, turbulent air from the aircraft in front passes into the following aircraft's engine intakes and disrupts the air flow through the compressor. This causes

the engine to cough and splutter, sometimes with a bang not unlike a supersonic boom and loud enough to be heard clearly on the ground, and there is usually a significant loss of thrust. The flame in the combustion chamber might be blown out causing the engine to spool down and rapidly lose thrust, but in this case the pilot will usually be able to re-light it without any trouble. Depending on engine indications, it is sometimes possible to continue with the sortie, but often the pilot will need to land as soon as possible just in case the engine has suffered damage. In the event of any emergency, however, the pilot's initial action must be to clear the formation.

Above all, the pilots have to learn to give 100 per cent concentration to the job in hand. As one of the pilots

Prior to every sortie, be it out of season practice, as in this case, or in-season display, there is a thorough and in-depth pre-flight briefing.

A Red Arrows' pilot, in addition to being a superb flyer, has to have the right temperament and personality, both from the point of view of successfully becoming a member of a close-knit team and of projecting the right image to the public. Andy 'Cubes' Cubin (Red 5) and Ian 'Smithy' Smith (Red 2) are quick to see the funny side as Gary 'Gazzer' Waterfall (Red 3) attempts to look suitably cool with his ice-cream.

put it, 'As soon as you let your concentration slip, something changes and then everything starts to go wrong.'

Each sortie is followed by a debriefing which can be anything up to 45-minutes in length. Every aspect of the flight is analysed and pilots are encouraged to criticise themselves as well as each other. The second and third year pilots give the FNGs the benefit of their own experience but are not above criticism themselves because they are flying in new positions and there is always something new to learn. Those visitors who are privileged to be allowed to sit in on a debriefing are usually astonished to find that the pilots will quibble about being just a couple of feet out of position. The pilots will frequently study individual frames of the video, or run the tape forwards and backwards in slow motion, to verify points of contention or to give advice to each other.

'Over the years the public have got used to the Red Arrows flying near perfect formations,' said Simon. 'If we don't strive for perfection from the very start, what do we strive for? When every pilot flies in exactly the right position, the Diamond Nine is perfectly symmetrical; but if one pilot is out of position by even a small amount, the whole shape looks wrong – and people will notice.'

Taking into account the time for briefing and debriefing, for getting to and from the aircraft, for taxiing out to the runway and taxiing back in again, means that each 30-minute flying slot actually uses up about two hours of the working day. With each pilot flying up to

The Boss, Squadron Leader Simon Meade, steps into the front office of his Hawk. Only after performing successfully in front of the Big Boss, Air Marshal Sir David Cousins, in a few days' time, will the Team be eligible to exchange their standard green flight suits for the coveted, tailored red versions.

three sorties per day there is little time left for hosting visitors, answering fan mail, and for all the other duties that any other RAF officer has to perform.

There is, for example, never time to repair to the Officers' Mess for lunch. The pilots have their midday meal in the crew room between sorties. To Ian Smith falls the privilege of stocking the refrigerator and organising the crew room and its facilities. Lunch tends to consist of sandwiches filled with a gooey mess concocted from the contents of whichever tins happen to come to hand. Tuna fish, sardines, strips of cheese, sliced meats, cold baked beans, pickles, and liberal dashes of Worcester or Tabasco sauces seem to be favoured ingredients. The selection is made by whichever of the pilots gets to the refrigerator first and the whole lot is then mashed together in a large mixing bowl. Generous helpings of the paste are spread on bread with a layer of low-fat margarine, supplemented by a variety of crisps supplied free of charge by a well-known local manufacturer, all washed down with copious quantities of coffee or tea. The coffee can be either instant – Gold Blend, naturally – or filter; the tea is usually a strange mixture of NAAFI's finest plus a dash of Earl Grey for added piquancy. For 'afters', Jaffa Cakes and Wagon Wheels tend to cancel out the beneficial properties of the low-fat margarine but are much tastier than the boring wholewheat biscuits for which Ian Smith has a predilection.

'Of course, we don't ask our visitors to eat the same food as we do,' said Ian. 'When we are hosting corporate visitors, we provide a finger buffet for them prepared in the Officers' Mess. Unfortunately, non-public funds do not provide much money for feeding visitors, so it's all a bit basic. The cash allowance works out at about £1 per head. That obviously doesn't go far but the Officers' Mess staff do their best for us.'

'It can be very embarrassing,' said Richie, who has seen it all before. 'When we go off on visits to the various companies that support the Team, or when we're invited into the hospitality suites at air displays, we're always given the VIP treatment and no expense is spared. Most of the visitors to our HQ understand that we're using taxpayers' money and that we shouldn't splash it around.'

At one such event, the Chief Executive of a major

UK company said, succinctly and unthinkingly as he helped himself to a cheese and tomato sandwich, 'It's nice to see that you chaps don't "posh it up" just because we're here!' There was a dreadful, silent moment as he realised the implication of his words, but to his chagrin the ground did not open up and swallow him. The incident was laughed off but not forgotten.

'Do the Red Arrows go back to their normal squadrons in the winter?' It is amazing how many people ask that question, or variations on the theme. In truth, the pilots probably work harder during the winter months than they do in the summer months when they are on the display circuit. Certainly anyone who sees the pilots in their crew room at the end of a good flying week in mid-winter, when they have flown three sorties per day for each of the five working days, will see nine supremely fit pilots thoroughly tired, both mentally and physically.

That's SOP too!

All strapped in and ready to roll, Flight Lieutenant Sean Perrett (Red 9) takes a moment to mentally prepare himself for the forthcoming practice display. In his third and final year with the Team, Sean will leave at the end of 1997, returning to RAF Wittering to fly Harriers.

FLT LT S D PERRETT
JNR TECH D P WEBSTER

ROYA

Getting into Sync!

'Synchro manoeuvres are made to look more dangerous than they actually are,' said Tim Couston cheerfully before his first practice, 'but even so they're no more dangerous than the rest of our flying. When we fly head-on towards each other we try to make it look exciting, but the manoeuvres are designed with safety in mind. One aircraft, the Synchro Leader, that's me, flies the predictable path and the other aircraft is responsible for the avoidance. It's as simple as that.

'Actually,' he added after a moment's thought, 'there is one refinement – we call it a fudge. To make it look to the punters on the ground as though we're exactly on a collision course, the aircraft furthest away from the crowd flies slightly higher than the other one. Because of the viewing angle this creates the optical illusion that we're at the same height. You can only see the height differential if you can get to a viewpoint at one end or the other of the display line – and you can't do that at most air displays.'

The concept of the Synchro Pair was born with the Yellow Jacks in 1964. Two soloists, flying synchronised manoeuvres alternating with the main section of five and later seven aircraft, have been an essential and very popular element of the second half of every Red Arrows' display since the Team's very first season. They not only give variety and added excitement to the display, but also contrast the graceful aerial ballet of the first half with much more dynamic manoeuvres.

The Synchro Pair did once have a spectacular and tragic accident. A favourite manoeuvre in the Red Arrows'

The nine immaculately prepared Red Arrows' Hawks taxi in formation for the Akrotiri runway. The last jet, with Air Commodore Gavin Mackay at the controls, is on a test flight.

early years was the Roulette which involves the two solo aircraft flying a complete 360-degree horizontal turn in opposite directions, crossing twice in front of the crowd. The combined closing speed is in the order of 800 mph. The geometry of the manoeuvre is such that for much of the time the two pilots cannot see each other and they have to rely on accurate flying with precise 'g' loadings and angles of bank, and split second assessments of the surface wind. Sadly, while practising the Roulette at Kemble on 20 January 1971, four pilots were killed when the Synchro Pair collided head-on. Each aircraft had one of the other Team members in the back seat. It was never established exactly what went wrong, partly because there was no video evidence in those days. For many years thereafter the Roulette was banned, but it has recently found its way back into the programme with additional safeguards.

The process of choosing the Synchro pilots is very democratic. Synchro Leader chooses his own number two from any of the first year pilots. Synchro 2 automatically becomes Synchro Leader the following year, his final year with the Team.

'I had two pilots to choose from,' explained Tim. 'Either of them could have done the job, but I chose Dave Stobie because he and I get on particularly well together – that's vitally important – and because I knew he would do a good job.'

'Of course I was disappointed,' said Andy Offer, the pilot not selected by Tim to be his number two. 'I knew I could do the job and I wanted it. A lot of people think that the synchro pilots are selected because they are the best – that's not correct. The fact is that any of us could do the job but Timmy and Dave go back a long way. I've always been a Harrier pilot so I know a different set of guys. I don't hold any sort of grudge against either of them.'

Stobes will have to make a similar decision at the end of the 1997 season. 'Of course, I'll have three pilots to choose from. I can't possibly say now who I will choose. I'll watch all three throughout the season and choose the

one I think is best fitted for the job. They'll have to be nice to me for a whole year,' he added with a grin.

'We work up our part of the show separately from the rest of the formation,' said Tim. 'We don't all get together until much later on. Traditionally Slot 1, 8 am take off, is given to the Synchro Pair. That means we have to get up very early and brief ourselves, but it also means that the rest of the pilots can stay in bed that little bit longer.'

Another reason for giving the first slot to the Synchro Pair is consideration for the ground crew. They have to come in earlier than the pilots, at 6.30, to open the hangar, tow the aircraft out on to the flight line and carry out the pre-flight preparations. When Synchro are flying the early slot, three aircraft are prepared – two to fly and one as a reserve. Only five ground crew are required for that.

Having been the solo Hawk Display Pilot in 1994, Stobes already had a lot of experience of flying low-level aerobatics. Nevertheless, before the two pilots were allowed to start flying together they each had to complete a number of low-level solo aerobatic sorties. Dave had to fly a series of individual sorties at ever reducing base heights. Before being cleared to each lower level, he had to be watched by, and have the approval of, both the Team Leader and the Commandant of the Central Flying School. Only then could he practice down to the minimum height of 100 feet above the ground right way up and a minimum of 150 feet inverted. He then had to fly four more sorties at those heights before the Pair were authorised to start practising together.

'The runway looks very large and seems to be rushing past at a great rate of knots when you see it from 150 feet, upside-down,' said Stobes after his first solo run at the lowest height. 'Of course, I'm not really looking at the runway surface; I'm looking straight ahead to the horizon – but you do get this very vivid impression!'

In the meantime Tim Couston had also been practising solo, polishing up his own aerobatics and working

out the routine he wanted to include in the 1997 display. On 31 October it was time for Tim to brief his number two for their first pairs sortie and, like all Red Arrows' briefings, it was not just a cosy chat in the crew room but a formal affair with an abundance of jargon.

'There'll be a standard procedure before each of our sorties, Dave. We'll start the briefing 30 minutes before take-off. I'll expect you to have obtained details of the local weather here and at the diversion airfield, the surface wind and 2,000-foot wind velocities, and get our aircraft numbers from the engineers. On this first sortie we'll carry out trimming runs to check that the aircraft fly properly whilst inverted. We'll fly those at 350 knots along the line of the runway. Keep well clear of me while we do that – there's no need to get very close. Then we'll

To ensure that everything runs smoothly in the maintenance department the Team take the majority of their support personnel out to Cyprus. Here some remedial attention is paid to the three smoke pipes located in the rear jet nozzle fairing.

try some line astern splits. Stay about two aircraft lengths behind me. If you get too high, you'll feel my wake on your rear end – you want to be just below that! When I call "split" it's smoke on, full power, full control deflection roll to the left and then pull to the light buffet to maintain a level turn. I go right, you go left.'

Light buffet is the gentle shaking of the whole airframe when the aircraft's wing is generating the maximum possible lift and just approaching the stalling angle of attack. The maximum rate of turn, very important for fighter pilots, is achieved at the light buffet and some pilots refer to this as being 'on the nibble'. Any further back pressure on the control column in an attempt to tighten the turn will take the aircraft into heavy buffet which is where the wing is completely stalled. If a pilot does fly his aircraft into heavy buffet, the turning performance deteriorates markedly, lift drops off dramatically and the aircraft may flick into a dangerous spin. The sudden loss of lift as the aircraft stalls means the aircraft will inevitably start to descend rapidly, the very last thing you want at low level. It needs a very precise touch to get it just right. Many of Synchro Pair's manoeuvres incorporate maximum rate turns and it often appears to observers on the ground that the aircraft is skidding around the turn. The pilots are subjected to up to eight times the force of gravity in such manoeuvres and that means every single part of the body, internal and external, appears to weigh eight times its normal weight.

'All Synchro's turns are initiated on the tone so we don't confuse the main section with unnecessary chat,' continued Tim. The tone is a 1,000 hertz bleep transmitted on the radio by a switch on the radio control box. The tone is quite distinctive and Dave will soon get used to acting as soon as he hears it.

'When we do the first head-on runs, you'll probably want to move further away from me. That will throw the pattern out. Don't worry; just fly to achieve your briefed line and I will be doing the same. And remember: we pass right-hand side to right-hand side.'

A very good point to remember!

For the start of the winter training season the Synchro Pair were allocated two 30-minute time slots overhead Cranwell, the early one at 8 am and the other mid-morning. The Cranwell slots are necessary so that Red Leader and the Commandant of the Central Flying School can supervise Tim and Dave from the ground. It would have been impracticable for Simon to drive to Scampton to watch the Synchro Pair and still have time

to lead his own three sorties. Synchro Pair's third daily slot is usually flown, unsupervised, overhead Scampton airfield in the early afternoon.

There are several small villages very close to Cranwell. Soon after the Synchro Pair started to practice, a small number of residents telephoned the Red Arrows' Public Relations Officer to complain about this unusual activity over their homes. For years Cranwell had been the home of flying training schools. Those aircraft tended to fly fairly slowly and sedately and were not often seen flying upside-down at high speed belching smoke!

In spite of what some complainants think, all complaints from the public about noise or low flying activities are taken seriously and are properly investigated to check whether any rules had been broken and to see if anything could be done to reduce the nuisance in the future. The video recording which is made of every practice at Cranwell and at Scampton, can be consulted if there is any doubt. While sympathising with the complainants, the PRO has to get across the message that the Red Arrows, and the Synchro Pair in particular, cannot avoid flying over every single home. Their manoeuvres are timed to the nearest second and turns have to be flown very precisely.

The Red Arrows orientate their activities around a location on the airfield known as Display Datum, a position representing where the VIP enclosure would be at an air display. At both Cranwell and Scampton, Display Datum is a point close to the Air Traffic Control tower. The entire display is flown with reference to that point and so the aircraft tend to follow the same path over the ground each time they fly. The airman with the video camera who records each practice or display for debriefing purposes, is always located exactly at Datum. At public displays the Team Manager will always position himself as close as possible to Datum.

When the pilots are planning a public show they place a transparent overlay of the standard display on a large-scale local area map in order to work out significant

had dropped well below zero again with the inevitable consequence that the airfield surfaces turned into sheets of ice. The thermometer remained stubbornly below zero all day Monday but, thanks to sterling efforts by the clearance team, the main runway at base was opened for flying from late morning. Unfortunately the low cloud base and poor visibility at Cranwell and all other UK air-fields, limited the Red Arrows' pilots to just a few solo sorties to regain their flying currency.

Clearing runways of snow and ice is a miserable, expensive, time-consuming and utterly frustrating task. If the clearance team is not ordered into action, pilots complain about engineers sitting around doing nothing. If the clearance team do their best but merely compact the snow and create vast sheets of ice, as often happens, the pilots make scathing remarks from the cosy warmth of their crew room – 'Same story every year, every time

It's 1 May 1997, and Public Display Authority (PDA) day. The Team must display before Air Marshal Sir David Cousins, who will determine whether it is of the required high standard and, as importantly, safe. With Sir David are Wing Commander Dick Johnston, Air Vice-Marshal Stables and Air Commodore Gavin Mackay.

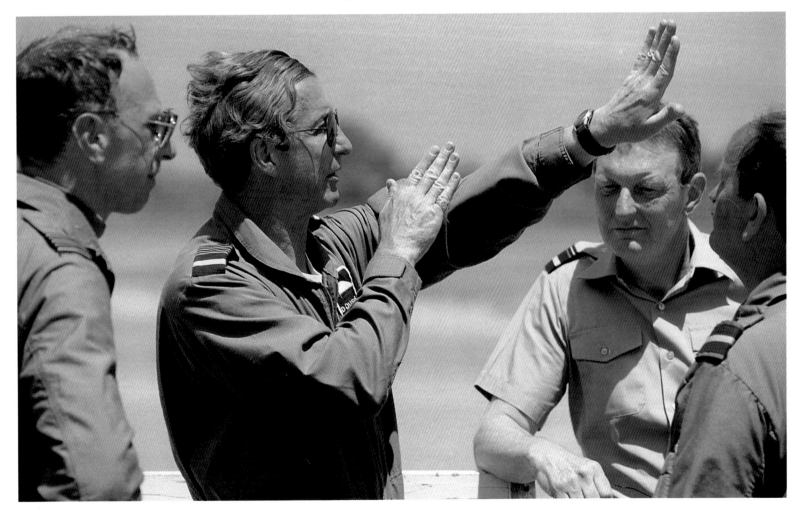

A perfectly positioned and executed Vixen Break finishes an equally perfect display, prompting Air Marshal Cousins to unhesitatingly pronounce the Red Arrows, Team '97, good to go.

there's an inch of snow the whole air force grinds to a halt!', 'When will they ever learn that it's better to leave it to clear naturally?', 'When I was operating out of Norway we . . .' – and so on.

Even the PRO joined in: 'I used to operate Victor Tankers out of Goose Bay in Labrador. The runway there was covered by several feet of compacted snow every winter. We just had to make sure the wingtips didn't strike the snow banks on either side of the runway!'

That remark prompted yawns all round and the conversation turned more interestingly to what Ian Smith and Andy Cubin had done in Hong Kong during their Christmas break.

The Team Leader insisted that there would be no formation practices over Scampton as long as the runway there remained unfit for emergency landings. The Scampton runway, taxiways and dispersals had not been touched since the first fall of snow and so were not safe for aircraft movements. This ruling led to some heated, but pointless, arguments.

'We don't want to land there – we just want to fly overhead.'

'We do plenty of displays that are not over airfields, so what?'

'Yes, but what if we *have* to land with an engine failure or something?' added someone else, prophetically as it happened.

The bad weather did not stop work in the Manager's department of the Squadron. Squadron Leader Mike Williams, Red 10, is now in his third and final year with the Team. He joined the RAF in 1975 and initially flew Victor Tanker aircraft on 57 Squadron from RAF Marham. He travelled widely with the Tanker Force and flew several air-to-air refuelling sorties during the Falklands Conflict. He later spent ten years flying Tornado GR1, including a number of operational missions during the Gulf War. Mange, pronounced with a short 'a' so as not to rhyme with the dog affliction, gives the commentary at all public displays and, at the same time, acts as a flight safety observer. He is in two-way radio contact with the Team Leader and can warn him of any potential hazards that might occur during a display. He also flies any cameramen who are given permission to film a display from the air. There is even a special ten-aircraft formation, known as 'Mange', used when the Team is in transit between airfields.

During the winter, the Manager runs the Squadron Operations Room. There is an Adjutant, Warrant Officer John Howard, and three clerks to assist him. The Manager is responsible, amongst many other things, for dealing with the RAF Participation Committee (PC). These civil servants, based at RAF Strike Command HQ in High Wycombe, prepare the programme of activities for all RAF display aircraft, not just the Red Arrows. The PC had produced the first draft of the Red Arrows' 1997 programme and delivered it to the Manager and Adjutant before the Christmas break so that they could start making plans. Anyone can write to the PC asking for a display by the Red Arrows and, in a typical year, several hundred show organisers do just that. There is nothing to stop private individuals writing in asking for displays or flypasts for village fêtes, weddings, or charity events.

Many people write and telephone direct to the Red Arrows, but all requests have to be passed on to the PC. The Red Arrows do not decide where they are going to fly, but they do have the final say about where and when displays are programmed. There is a whole raft of operating parameters that have to be taken into account and the PC are not qualified to make such decisions. The Hawk is a relatively short-range aircraft and so the display location, if it is not the airfield from which the Team is operating, needs to be within 80 nautical miles of the operating airfield. As a general rule the Team will not fly more than two displays on any given day. If there are long transit flights to get from one location to another, only one display per day will be programmed. It is not just the pilots who get tired; the ground crew, the often forgotten army, start work before the pilots and finish after them.

It's with a measure of relief and a high degree of pride and happiness that, at last, those rather unflattering green suits can be traded in for the well-earned and much-prized red ones.

The Team have been working flat out, but now it's time to relax a little and take a short break. There's no flying tomorrow, and that's probably wise, for tonight brings the Red Suit Party – for very special guests only!

Displays organisers almost always want the Red Arrows either to open their show or to close it. They know that if the Red Arrows are on first, the crowds will come early; if the Red Arrows are on last, the crowds will stay to the end. Keeping the spectators at the air show as long as possible is a major aim of all display organisers because the longer people stay at the show, the more money they will spend. Sometimes the display organiser and the crowds get a little extra for their money. This happens when the Team is landing at the display site before their display, or taking off from the site after their display to move on elsewhere. Such movements have to be carefully programmed into the flying programme; the Red Arrows cannot land or take off when other aircraft are displaying overhead.

It seems to come as a surprise to many people to learn that the Team needs a day off occasionally! In early January the operations board already showed that from April, Team members would be away from home on 24 out of 26 consecutive weekends. Inevitably, most air shows are organised for weekends, but organisers of the smaller shows have learned that they stand a better chance of getting the Red Arrows if they fix their event for days other than Saturdays, Sundays and Bank Holidays. In the busiest months, July and August, it is not uncommon for the Red Arrows to be working on ten or 11 consecutive days.

The Red Arrows do not come free. A full 25-minute display costs in the order of £6,000, including the mandatory insurance premium and VAT, but the Team members are always quick to point out that they do not get the money! The algorithm for calculating the fee is rather tortuous and goes something like this. The RAF Aerobatic Team is established to give about 100 public displays each year. The RAF Budget pays for that. However, the tax-payer should not have to pay for the extra travel and subsistence costs that arise from the necessity of moving the team around the country to display sites. Those additional costs are averaged out and each show organiser pays one share. This fee is of little

The next day there's time to catch up on a bit of admin and, while Andy 'Offo' Offer puts in a call to his stockbroker (!), Stobes, Smithy and Gazzer personalise a few limited edition lithographs.

consequence to the organisers of the largest shows. If they are charging £10 for entry, and many charge more than that, they only need 600 punters to offset the entire cost of the Red Arrows' appearance. The fee is more of a problem for the small show organisers and that is why flypasts are popular.

Straight flypasts are free but can only be authorised when the Team is passing by and is able to carry out the flypast without any significant deviation from the planned course. Organisers of local events have learned how to exploit this. They find out when and where the Red Arrows will be performing at a nearby air show and then arrange their local event to coincide.

Whenever the Team is transiting between airfields and displays at low level and in sight of the ground, they always fly in a tidy formation. Thus, if people on the ground see the Team passing over, they will see an orderly formation rather than an undisciplined gaggle. This leads to some surprising, sometimes touching, letters. In the last 12 months there have been three serendipitous events. There was the lady who wrote to thank the Team for flying over her husband's funeral, at the precise moment of the interment. When she asked who had arranged the flypast for her husband, an ardent fan, the PRO could only reply, reverently and sincerely, 'It must

The children at a local schools' football competition brimmed with excitement when they learned that Simon Meade was going to hand out the prizes.

have been an act of God.' Then there was the flypast over the 18th green at a Midlands golf course just as the Lady Captain was receiving her farewell gift at the end of her term of office; and the couple in Essex who were treated to a flypast as they stood on the steps of the Registry Office posing for photographers just after their wedding.

For the rest of that first week in 1997 the freezing conditions persisted and Scampton airfield remained black. The pilots started to get bored with the enforced inactivity. One day they went off to the swimming pool to carry out the mandatory annual dinghy drills and the next day they went to the gymnasium to carry out their annual fitness tests. At the Friday Met Briefing, the Duty Forecaster promised that milder conditions were on the way. He was right. There were three days of excellent flying weather at the start of the second week and several seven-aircraft practices were flown, with Synchro Pair for the first time flying in their proper slots behind the Leader. These sorties were known as Left-Hand Sides or Right-Hand Sides depending on which pilots were not flying.

Then fate took a hand and there was a near disaster.

Bird Strike!

'There I was, working hard, when all of a sudden there was the most enormous bang followed by a huge increase in cockpit noise.'

That was how Ian Smith described the start of a frightening incident that happened on 21 January at 350 miles an hour, 400 feet above open farm land north west of Scampton, towards the end of a routine practice by six aircraft.

'I realised immediately from the draught and the noise that the canopy over my head had disintegrated and I immediately thought that I'd had a bird strike although that was not the only possibility. Instinctively I went for my escape route – I rolled my wings level and eased upwards out of the formation towards the cloud base. Until that moment all my attention had been concentrated on watching the leader through the left-hand side of my cockpit.'

Whenever something dramatic and possibly hazardous happens to a military fast jet aircraft at low level, the first imperative is to 'fly the aircraft'. There is no point in diagnosing the problem only to find that the aircraft has gone out of control in the meantime. When the Red Arrows are in close formation, any pilot in trouble has to fly his aircraft and take it expeditiously out of the formation, following the pre-briefed escape route, so that other aircraft in the formation are not put in danger. The second imperative with a single-engined aircraft such as the Hawk is to conserve energy by converting excess air speed into height. In the event of damage to, or complete failure of, the single engine, height above the ground is vitally important. In still air, a Hawk with total engine failure can glide, at best, two nautical miles for every 1,000 feet loss of altitude. In such a predicament, the more height the pilot can gain, the more time he has to assess the situation. He must decide whether to abandon

the aircraft by using his ejection seat or attempt to fly to a suitable airfield for an emergency landing. He must consider the cloud base and visibility. It is not a good idea to fly deliberately into cloud because he would then have the added problem of making a safe descent back down through the cloud.

In the first five seconds after the canopy disintegrated Ian had a lot to think about and a lot of important decisions to make.

'I had a very good idea of where we were in relation to Scampton airfield and I knew that the cloud base was quite low,' said Ian. 'I didn't want to pull back too hard on the control column because that would have taken me straight into the cloud. I also knew I didn't have to worry

It is amazing the damage that can be caused to a jet aircraft by a small bird when the closing speed is around 350 mph. The hole punched into the nose of Ian Smith's Hawk indicates the impact point of just one of five lapwings.

about where the other aircraft were in relation to me; it was the Boss's responsibility to keep them out of my way and I knew I could trust him to do that. When I looked into the cockpit to see what indications I had on the instruments, I realised that I had virtually no visibility through the front windscreen because of blood and gore on the outside. That confirmed I'd had a massive bird strike. I couldn't hear anything on the radio because of the noise – it was quite overwhelming. Strangely, I remember feeling quite alone – we get so used to being able to talk to each other and to the controllers on the ground – but when I saw Red 4 alongside me I knew that someone knew I was in trouble. Now it was up to me to sort things out.'

Andy Offer takes up the story. 'We were just completing a left-hand turn towards Scampton airfield, preparatory to running in for a flat break. I saw a large flock of birds and I just had time to think, "we're going to hit them" when I saw them strike Smithy's aircraft. I saw his canopy disintegrate and I clearly saw loads of blood streaming over the front windscreen. My first thought was that the blood was Smithy's but he gave me a thumbs up and I knew then that he was OK. He eased upwards out of the formation and I stayed with him. Almost immediately I could see that the whole of the top part of his canopy had disappeared. I called the Leader and told him that Ian had had a bird strike and had lost his canopy. I knew that Ian would not be able to transmit or hear anything on his radio because of the high noise level.'

The Controller on duty in the Tower at Scampton, Sergeant Carl Stevens, saw two aircraft pull up and out of the formation. As soon as he heard Andy Offer's radio message, he immediately alerted the crash, fire and ambulance crews for an emergency landing.

Although he did not know it at the time, Ian's aircraft had flown through a flock of lapwings. One or more birds had entered the engine intakes causing extensive damage to the compressor blades, while other birds had damaged the nose section, the centreline smoke pod, the mainplane and the tailplane. At least one bird had struck the thick Perspex canopy above Ian's head, causing it to shatter, thus, as one of the pilots wryly put it afterwards, converting the aircraft to a 'Hawk Cabriolet'. Some pieces of the broken Perspex ended up in the cockpit and damaged Ian's flying helmet. Curiously, other pieces managed to get between Ian's back and the ejection seat,

causing rips to the fabric. Ian's helmet and flying suit were spattered with blood.

'All the engine instruments seemed to be OK and the aircraft was flying normally,' continued Ian. 'However, bird strikes like that almost always cause damage to the engine even if nothing untoward shows up on the instruments. By this time, and it was only a few seconds since the strike, I was overhead Scampton with plenty of speed in hand. I decelerated and positioned the aircraft for a precautionary landing – that means I flew the pattern in such a way that if the engine had suddenly packed in I would still have enough height and speed to reach the runway safely. I knew there was a small village on the final approach and I had already decided that if anything else went seriously wrong at that late stage I would point the aircraft away from the village towards the open ground and eject. Fortunately that was not necessary.'

As soon as the damaged Hawk came to rest, the crash crews surrounded the aircraft. They were probably a little disappointed that there was no need to cover the area with foam, nor were they required to rescue the pilot from the cockpit since he had climbed out unaided.

Once Red Leader, watching from his vantage point in orbit over the airfield, saw that Ian's aircraft was clear of the runway, he instructed Andy Cubin to land and pick Ian up. Then the remaining four aircraft turned south and returned to Cranwell. About an hour after the incident, Andy and Ian landed at base in the serviceable Hawk. The emergency personnel moved the damaged Hawk into the Red Arrows' former hangar at Scampton to await a party of servicing personnel.

The two local radio stations and the local newspapers usually get hold of dramatic stories about aircraft very quickly; there is almost always someone on the spot ready to phone in to the news rooms. When this incident occurred, the chief public relations officer from Command Headquarters just happened to be on a visit to the Red Arrows. The Team's PRO had a little bet with him that

Training is complete and now the Red Arrows can get on with what they do best – thrilling audiences at air displays. Once back in the UK, their first public appearance is at the North Weald Show and, on rather a blustery day, Reds 8 and 9 trail red smoke as they fly beneath the stepped-up Goose formation.

(Previous page) From the southern end of England, it's up to bonnie Scotland for a display amid the rather overcast but nevertheless very beautiful scenery that surrounds the famous Gleneagles Hotel.

(Above) Every display is recorded on video for analysis at the obligatory debrief. The morning after the Gleneagles show, time is made to look at each manoeuvre in detail. The Team continually strive to match their motto – Eclat, Excellence.

within minutes one of the news editors would telephone asking for more information. For once the PRO was wrong: no one seemed to have noticed anything untoward.

After an initial inspection of the damaged Hawk, the engineers were certain that nothing other than pieces of Perspex had fallen from it. The pieces were probably no larger than six to eight inches across and were unlikely to have caused damage or injury because they would be very light in weight. However, the pieces would contain segments of miniature detonating cord – MDC. MDC is fitted between layers of both front and rear canopies and is used to shatter the canopy immediately prior to a pre-meditated ejection, thereby leaving a clear route out of the aircraft for the ejection seat. The MDC is fired by a small electric current. The engineers were sure that any MDC inside fragments of Perspex found on the ground would be completely inert.

At each display it's the Team Manager's job to both commentate and note any potential hazards. Squadron Leader Mike Williams – the 'Mange' – gets a lift to Southend in a Gazelle helicopter, using the opportunity, as we approach, to familiarise himself with the site layout.

The Team's PRO contacted the local police head-quarters in Gainsborough to tell them about the incident and the Duty Officer there agreed to inform the Red Arrows if anyone called in to report falling debris. The following day a 20-strong party of airmen was sent out to brief the landowners about the incident and to comb a four square kilometre area of farmland for pieces of Perspex. They searched from dawn to dusk across fields knee-deep in mud but found nothing.

The Red Arrows' technicians quickly determined that the damage to the Hawk was quite extensive. It would not be practicable to make the aircraft serviceable to fly out of Scampton so they started to dismantle it. In the following days they took the wings off the aircraft, not an operation that pilots like to watch, and loaded the crippled Hawk on to a low-loader for the 25-mile journey down the A15, through the centre of Lincoln, to Cranwell.

For many years the Red Arrows' ground crew had been divided into two flights – first and second line. First Line dealt with the aircraft on the daily flying programme

The display at Southend is located on the sea front. Being public land it's free, attracting hundreds of thousands of visitors. Picnickers enjoy the sun and the spectacle as the Red Arrows fly past in Diamond Nine.

while Second Line had responsibility for the aircraft undergoing routine maintenance in the hangar. Eng 1 and Eng 2 were the engineering officers in charge of each flight.

'It was an inefficient system,' explained Flight Lieutenant Dick Burn. Dick had been Eng 2 with the Red Arrows since March 1995. He had missed out on the overseas tours to Africa and the Far East because he was the Project Officer for the move from Scampton and was needed at base to make all the logistics arrangements. Dick is a gentle giant, 6ft 5ins tall and 105 kgs, well respected, socially and professionally, by everyone who comes into contact with him. He has represented the RAF at both Rugby and Judo.

'We used to juggle airframe flying hours on our 11 aircraft so that most of the scheduled maintenance tasks fell due in the winter months. During the latter stages of each winter, when the Boss wanted to start flying nine aircraft at a time, we had to borrow Hawks from other stations to compensate for the three or four of our own aircraft that were still in the hangar. The aviation photographers used to like that because they could get pic-

The previous day's display was in the evening – and a beautiful one it was too, as the Team initiate their display, flying in, as ever, from crowd rear in Big Nine.

tures of the Team flying aircraft in a variety of paint schemes. However, that system more or less guaranteed that we would have ten aircraft serviceable to fly on every day during the display season.'

Because more technicians were required on Second Line in the winter than in the summer to cope with the extra work, it meant that airmen kept shifting from one flight to the other. It was quite unsettling for them but the advantage was that each pilot always – or almost always – flew the same aircraft. That is important because every airframe has its individual idiosyncrasies and pilots get used to them. When the Team moved from Scampton to Cranwell, an extra two aircraft were added to the inven-

tory, aircraft that had until then been used by Hawk-qualified staff officers and examiners of the Central Flying School. This gave the engineers the opportunity they had been waiting for to reorganise the Squadron and bring it into line with normal RAF practice.

'I was the Project Officer for the change,' continued Dick. 'I recommended that we should no longer have two separate flights. All the airmen would belong

With red smoke trailing and air brake flailing, Synchro Leader Tim Couston accelerates in for a dramatic head to head pass with Synchro Two, Dave Stobie.

to one flight and come under the direct control of a junior engineering officer. In this way, the Jengo would have control over all the airmen and would be able to allocate them as required. The other engineering officer, to be known as Sengo, senior engineering officer, would be responsible for the whole of the engineering policy and management. Under this new organisation, which was brought into effect at the start of the year, the Squadron should be able to carry out all scheduled

maintenance as and when it becomes due throughout the year and this will permit much more efficient use of manpower. The downside is that the pilots will not be able to fly their own airframe on every occasion. At any given time during the year there will be two aircraft on scheduled maintenance. The pilots'll have to learn to live with that.'

A week after the bird strike, Flight Lieutenant Dick Burn was posted, at very short notice, to take up a new appointment as a senior engineering officer on a Tornado station with well-deserved promotion to Squadron Leader. Flight Lieutenant Dave Chowns was posted in as the new Sengo. He had spent the last four years just up the road at Waddington, where he was working on the

As the sun descends on Southend, smoking Reds 8 and 9 – alias Richie Matthews and Sean Perrett – mimic the widely spanned twin engines of the Sukhoi SU-27 in Flanker Bend.

Sentry Airborne Early Warning aircraft. He had also been the engineering officer for the famous and much-loved Vulcan display aircraft at Waddington in the last six months before it was taken out of service.

'When I was at school in Bury St Edmunds I used to go to the Mildenhall Air Show every year to see the Red Arrows,' said Dave. 'I've been volunteering to serve on the Red Arrows for a number of years and now I'm looking forward to the challenge and to fulfilling a long-held ambition.'

Eight days after the bird strike, while Dick was in the process of handing over to Dave Chowns, one of the local newspapers, acting on a tip-off, telephoned the PRO to ask about the incident, thus beginning a whole series of media stories starring Ian Smith. All of a sudden, Ian was a blood-spattered hero and he received telephone calls from friends all over the country asking after his well-being. He was not to know then that the story had still not run its full course.

No pieces of Perspex were ever found – at least, no one handed any in. No one enquired about the lapwings: the Bird Control Officer at Scampton was concerned about them – but for statistical purposes only. He was no doubt relieved that the incident had taken place well outside his area of responsibility. Dave Chowns was blissfully unaware that his first challenge would present itself on his very first day.

On Friday 31 January, when Dick Burn had barely left the station, all the Hawks world-wide were grounded.

The Mange, Squadron Leader Mike Williams, also a skilled and experienced fast jet pilot, tucks the spare tenth Hawk in close on the transit flight from Leuchars in Scotland to Mildenhall.

Grounded!

'I couldn't believe it was happening to me,' said Dave Chowns on 3 February, his first Monday morning with the Red Arrows. 'When they rang me up to say all the aircraft were in effect grounded, I thought it was a bit of Red Arrows' banter for the new boy. But it was true. Apparently a potentially serious fault was discovered in one of the Hawk's powered control units (PCUs) during routine maintenance on one of the aircraft at Valley. There are three similar hydraulic-operated PCUs in each Hawk, one for each aileron and another for the tail plane. The fault was discovered when one of the units was undergoing routine bay servicing at Valley. Because the components are critical for safe flight, the RAF's Chief Engineer had no alternative but to require all similar units to be inspected before the next flight.'

Unfortunately, it is not possible to test the PCUs when they are installed in aircraft. It takes a pair of skilled technicians one and a half hours to dismantle and remove each item, another two hours to reinstall it and then they have to carry out functional tests in situ, altogether a minimum of ten hours per aircraft. But that was not all. Once the units had been removed from the aircraft, each one had to undergo non-destructive testing (NDT) in the hydraulics bay. First, however, a test routine had to be devised because this type of failure had never occurred before.

The component that had failed at Valley had easily been identified on a visual inspection because an operating lever inside the PCU had almost disintegrated. The RAF engineers decided that NDT would be needed to detect any latent problems early, long before they would be visible to the naked eye. The scheme they devised employed ultrasonics, not dissimilar to the scans used for unborn babies. Any microscopic defects in the metal would show up on the test equipment. There were three

Celebrity status goes hand-in-hand with the red suit and wherever they go, admiring autograph hunters, particularly (but not necessarily) of the younger variety, are sure to follow.

centres in the RAF that had suitable facilities for carrying out the delicate NDT, one of them, conveniently, being at Cranwell, but with over 100 Hawks in service

The Mildenhall show is one of the biggest events in the Team's calendar, particularly as they actually operate out of the USAF base in front of the crowd. Sir Richard Johns, Chief of the Air Staff, chats informally with the Team.

with the RAF, it was clearly going to be a long process getting them all back in the air.

The pilots were scheduled for routine simulator training at Valley that Monday morning. Normally they would have flown themselves in Hawks, but on this occasion they had to hitch a lift in one of Cranwell's Jetstream training aircraft. As it happens, the first three days of that week produced some of the best flying weather of the year, almost spring-like with brilliant blue skies. The pilots found it extremely frustrating having to sit on the ground.

The first Red Arrows' Hawk, indeed the first Hawk in the RAF, was ready to fly by mid-morning on the Wednesday. Sean Perrett was programmed to fly it on an air test but, unfortunately and to the great frustration of all the engineers, the aircraft developed a fuel leak totally unconnected with the NDT. To add to the frustration, the PCUs in Sean's aircraft were the first ones that had been removed, tested and declared free from defect. Because other aircraft were waiting for serviceable PCUs, Sean's aircraft had to be cannibalised so that the PCUs could be

Simon and Sean check and double-check datum and run in. Mildenhall attracts tens of thousands of hardened air show 'experts', so a good performance is essential.

transferred to another aircraft. Several more lost hours!

The media did not get to hear of the PCU problem until a story appeared in *The Times* on Wednesday 5 February although, with a fine regard for semantics, RAF senior engineers insisted that the fleet was not 'grounded'. The local media in the Cranwell area picked up on the story after that, but by then aircraft were slowly coming back into service. There was little visual appeal for television directors and, because no drama was involved, the media quickly dropped the story.

Meanwhile, the Red Arrows' ground crew were still trying to come to terms with their new working environment. Collectively they are known as 'the Blues' because they wear royal blue flying suits when they appear in public. People sometimes ask, 'Why don't the ground crew wear red suits like the pilots and the engineers?' 'Well, we couldn't call them the Blues if they wore red suits, could we!' Unquestionably true.

For many years it had been a tradition that Eng 1 wore a red flying suit – the only non-pilot to be accorded that distinction. The privilege was granted so that the

engineer would be readily recognised away from base as being part of the Red Arrows. The wearing of the distinctive red suit with a Red Arrows' name tag opens many doors. Under the new management structure, the pilots had agreed that both engineering officers should be allowed to wear red suits. Dick Burn would have had the largest red suit ever made and there were plenty of crew room jokes about whether the Team budget could afford it. Sadly, before Dick's suit was completed, word came through of his posting and work on his suit was immediately abandoned.

The Hawk Mark 1 and 1A aircraft used by the Red Arrows are two-seaters with full dual controls. When the Team flies transit sorties, the back seats are usually occupied by selected ground tradesmen. These airmen are known as the Circus, possibly a reference to Sir Alan Cobham's Flying Circus of the 1930s, but no one seems to know.

'When we fly away for displays elsewhere, we take ten aircraft,' explained Jon Russell, the Jengo. 'The tenth aircraft is flown by the Team Manager and is then available as a reserve in case one of the others becomes unserviceable. On long overseas tours we try to take 11 aircraft just to give us a little more flexibility. I fly in one back seat and that leaves nine more back seats for the Circus. The eleventh aircraft, when there is one, usually has two spare pilots in it.'

The Circus personnel are selected so that there is a

good cross-section of trades represented. Between them, the Circus should be able to deal with all turn-round servicings and minor unserviceabilities that might crop up. If the Team is going to operate away from base for several sorties, additional servicing personnel and spare parts are deployed either by road or, for overseas sorties, in a support Hercules.

Sergeant Brent Hall is the 1997 Circus Leader. He has worked continuously on Hawks since his first tour in the RAF in 1982 apart from a two year stint on Nimrods to break up the sequence. Circus Leader is almost always the previous year's deputy Circus Leader. All the airmen who fly in the circus have to be volunteers because the

Just how late can I leave it? As Red 9 completes the donning of his flight gear, Red 4 casually examines his watch. Offo always likes to leave it as late as possible, likes to be the last to strap in – it's one of those macho fighter pilot things!

RAF cannot compel non-aircrew to fly regularly, other than as passengers in transport aircraft. There is never any shortage of volunteers.

'I was actually posted to a corporal's slot on the Red Arrows in 1990 but before I got to Scampton to join the Team I was promoted to sergeant and that posting was changed,' said Brent. 'Instead I stayed on at Chivenor for another four years. When I joined the Team three years ago I hoped to get the Circus Leader's job because I wanted to fly. In the display season, I go wherever the Team goes; in the winter months I run the flight line operations and train up the new Circus guys.'

Each airman normally spends two years on the Circus. That's partly to give others an opportunity and also because it's extremely hard work. The Circus start work before the pilots and finish after them. They spend as much time away from home and family as the pilots. The Circus Leader, in conjunction with Jengo, picks the new circus members.

'We take it for granted that those who get on to the short list are fully competent at their professional job,' said Brent. 'What we're looking for are reliable, conscientious team workers – guys who can be trusted to get on with the job without close supervision all the time.'

Each member of the circus has to pass an annual aircrew-style medical examination and each has to undergo decompression training at the Aviation Medicine Training Centre at North Luffenham in Rutland. The air-

Ice Cool Cubes. If the boys were nervous about their first major public display, they certainly didn't show it. Andy Cubin strikes a quick pose for the photographer.

men have to be fit enough and knowledgeable enough to cope with any emergencies that might occur during high level transit flying. Additionally, they have to undergo the same ejection seat, dinghy and parachute training drills as the pilots. There is no point strapping yourself into an ejection seat unless you know instinctively how to operate it if the need arises.

'The Circus have to learn a lot of extra skills outside their main trade speciality,' continued Brent. 'For example, they have to know how to "prep" the aircraft for the pilot – on all other RAF squadrons the pilots do their own walk-round and pre-flight checks. On the Red Arrows the Circus do them for their pilot to save time.

With pilots all aboard (including Red 4), they swelter in the hot Suffolk sun awaiting their precise start-up time. In front, the blues stand smartly to attention. On start-up, their ground safety checks will be carried out in precise unison.

It's a very responsible part of the job. Then they have to learn how to pack the spares into the few spaces in the aircraft. We have to carry all the aircraft intake blanks and the wheel chocks so that they are available to make the aircraft secure as soon as we land. There is also a small pannier into which the airman and the pilot have to squeeze their overnight kit. If you watch the Red

To infinity and beyond! Sean Perrett taps his mascot, Buzz Lightyear, on the head, just for luck. Standing proudly on Red 9's cockpit coaming, Buzz was awarded a grandstand view at every display flown by the Team in 1997.

Arrows operating at an away base, you will see that the Circus guy is always first out of the aircraft after landing and the last on board before departure.'

Being on the Circus is not always as glamorous as people imagine and it can be downright frustrating. When the Red Arrows visited Victoria Falls in Zimbabwe in the autumn of 1995, the ground crew were the only members of the party who did not see the Falls from the ground. It was dark when they got to their hotel after servicing the Hawks and it was dark the following morning when they left the hotel to drive the 50 kms back to the airport to prep the aircraft for the onward flight. The Circus did, however, see the Falls from the air when the Team made a couple of flypasts before landing.

Each member of the Circus flies with the same pilot throughout the season. Jengo chooses his aircraft, Red 8 this year. Circus Leader always flies with the Team Leader and the deputy Circus Leader with Synchro Leader, Red 6. This allocation ensures that if two sec-

tions of aircraft ever get separated there is always a engineering supervisor on the ground. The Team's video operator always flies with the Team Manager because they work together on the ground at the air displays. The other six back seats are allocated in consultation with the pilots.

For 'see-offs' in front of the public, the Circus endeavour to synchronise their actions although they do not try to emulate the very formal and precise drill movements used by the American display teams. Once he has helped his pilot to strap into the ejection seat, the Circus man moves to the nose of the aircraft. When the pilot is ready to close the aircraft canopy, the air-

man turns his back. This is for his own protection. As the canopy locks into the down position, there is a slight possibility that the MDC might fire. This actually happened in 1990 just as the Team were getting ready to depart from Scampton for their tour of the Soviet Union. On that occasion the MDC fired accidentally as the pilot closed the canopy. Pieces of shattered Perspex were scattered all across the flight line at Scampton, some pieces travelling as much as 200

(Left) Reds 6 and 7, Tim Couston and Dave Stobie, are accomplished masters at making the safe look unsafe. It's all a question of angles and relative positions.

Smoke 'em! Taxiing in at the back of the line of jets, Red 9, Sean Perrett, likes nothing more than to smoke the unsuspecting. Deftly slewing his jet through 90 degrees, the (up until then) gesturing Patrouille Suisse team receive Sean's inevitable and unavoidable reply. Game, set and match, methinks!

metres. Because the Circus man had his back to the aircraft, he was not injured by the flying pieces but had he been facing the aircraft it would have been quite a different story.

After the engine has started, each pilot checks the hydraulic systems, flaps, airbrake and flying controls. The Circus man checks that the control surfaces are moving in the correct direction and finally checks for hydraulic leaks. After a final thumbs up to the pilot, the airman about turns and waits by the nose of his aircraft, watching for a signal from Circus Leader standing centrally some 30 metres in front of the line of aircraft. On that signal, all the airmen march out together about 20 metres, about turn to face the aircraft again and wait for the aircraft to start taxiing.

The aircraft taxi out in numerical order. The aircraft

Time for a smattering of entente cordiale, as Simon chats aerobatic talk with Major Vincent Cousin, leader of the superb Patrouille de France.

should have been parked in such a way that as each pilot turns on to the taxiway, the aircraft's jet pipe points away from the line of aircraft. This is to avoid foreign object damage (FOD) caused by the jet wash from one aircraft blowing dust and loose articles from the taxiway into the engine intake of the following aircraft.

With the help of technicians brought in from other RAF stations at Leeming, St Athan and Coningsby, all the Red Arrows' aircraft had been checked by the evening of Monday 10 February. None of the PCUs taken from Red Arrows' aircraft was faulty. Indeed, by this time the Engineering Staff at RAF Logistics Command had been able to check their records and could report that there had been no previously recorded instance of this particular fault in the 700,000 flying hours that the RAF's Hawks had amassed since entering service 20 years ago.

Once all the Red Arrows' Hawks had been cleared for flight following the PCU checks, the pilots and ground crew started looking forward to the first nine-ship formation – but there was more frustration still to come.

All Aboard!

'The first time we fly all nine pilots together is a very significant occasion,' said Simon in an interview on BBC Radio Lincolnshire. 'It's not that it's more difficult to fly all nine together, but when they've done it, the FNGs suddenly feel that they belong. The first nine-ship also signals the beginning of the end of the training season and we all look forward to that.'

The first nine aircraft formation it usually flown in mid- to late-January, but the combination of adverse weather, pilot sickness and aircraft availability delayed this crucial sortie by some six or seven weeks.

For much of the second week in February the pilots were grounded again. This time it was not aircraft unserviceability but the weather that caused the frustration. Gale-force south-westerly winds, gusting at times up to 55 knots over much of England, kept the Hawks on the ground. The problem does not lie entirely with the aircraft. It matters little to the airframe whether the surface wind is calm or blowing at 50 knots – as long as the direction is along the runway. A 50 knot headwind down the runway means the aircraft has an airspeed of 50 knots even before the pilot releases the brakes and that gives a considerably reduced take off run. A strong crosswind component can make directional control of the aircraft difficult and eventually impossible. Gusting winds also lead to considerable turbulence at low level and that makes close formation flying very difficult. However, the major consideration is the pilots' safety in the event of an ejection. Landing by parachute in a 50 knot wind is akin to jumping off the top of a bus while travelling at 50 knots and likely to be just as damaging.

Just as Ian Smith was getting over his fright and his fame, a well-known national Sunday newspaper got hold of the story and decided they wanted to make a splash, albeit a delayed one. One Friday afternoon in late February, four weeks after the bird strike, a reporter and photographer arrived at the Squadron HQ to interview Smithy and he had to re-live the experience all over again. It has to be said, however, that time had not dimmed Ian's memory. The newspaper devoted two full pages to the story and dramatised it to the full. No one could say that the story was inaccurate, but the 'horrified villagers who watched the stricken jet streaking over their heads' certainly never made themselves known to the RAF. As a result of that story two regional TV companies came to do their own version. Smithy spent much of another weekend answering the telephone! The *Readers' Digest* and the BBC TV programme *999* both subsequently contacted the PRO with a view to doing items about the bird strike but, to Ian's great relief, both decided not to proceed.

On 26 February, having passed a medical board, Richie Matthews went, with understandable trepidation, to RAF North Luffenham for a decompression test. He passed with flying colours. The following day he flew with the Team, his first sortie since 8 December. The day after that the Red Arrows flew five aircraft, all that were serviceable, in a salute for the President of Israel as he stepped from his aircraft at the start of a one-day State Visit to Cranwell. The Hawks trailed blue and white smoke, the Israeli national colours, and later the President met the Team Leader and some of the pilots at a static display in a hangar.

A series of unrelated technical problems continued to thwart Simon's wish to fly a nine-aircraft formation. In the first week of March, the CFS Examiners came to fly individual handling sorties with the pilots. Other special visitors early in the month included Simon Weston, the Gulf War hero, who had won a VIP day out at Cranwell at a charity auction, and the then Minister of State for the

Armed Forces, the Hon Nicholas Soames MP. Mr Soames listened sympathetically to the Team's problems with their 'temporary' accommodation at Cranwell and said that we could expect a further announcement about the Team's future permanent home in the summer.

More thick fog disrupted the flying programme in the week beginning 10 March, but then things started to look up. The weather was not perfect on the morning of Friday 14 March, but there was a reasonably high cloud base with light winds and no fog or precipitation – and all the pilots were fit to fly. Now the only factor that could delay the big event would be the lack of nine serviceable aircraft. There was a palpable air of expectation in the crew room when the pilots and engineers gathered for the morning briefing. Everyone knew that the Boss wanted to fly the first nine-ship formation and that this could be the day.

Two of the officers had a financial interest in the date of the big one. Some weeks earlier Dave Chowns had bet Andy Offer half a day's pay that the first nine would be flown on or before 14 March. A squadron leader's pay including flying pay is considerably more that a flight lieutenant engineer's pay but Andy's money had seemed safe right up until the last day.

'Nine,' announced Jengo, his shortest briefing ever. The monosyllable was greeted with a cheer. The nine included two loan aircraft, an all-black one from Llanbedr near Valley and the other from the Station Flight at RAF St Athan in South Wales.

'Then we'll fly nine; briefing at 8.40,' said Simon, thereby breaking another Red Arrows' tradition. In previous years, the first nine-ship had been flown in the last slot of the day so that a small champagne party could be held with the wives immediately after landing. At the back of his mind was the thought that if he flew less than nine aircraft on the first two sorties of the day there might not be nine serviceable for the third sortie. In any case he judged the pilots to be ready.

'We're not airborne yet,' said Andy with a sickly grin towards Dave, who was already gleefully rubbing fingers and thumb together in money-counting fashion.

On the face of it, the pre-flight briefing was much like any other briefing apart from the fact that all nine model aircraft were positioned on the magnetic board. The FNGs seemed the most hyped and could barely conceal their excitement. The second and third year pilots had seen it all before but even they found it difficult to contain their enthusiasm. This sortie had been a long time coming. Simon's job was to curb the exuberance and ensure that his pilots calmed down before they strapped into their aircraft.

'This will be a display take off, coming right when airborne.' Nothing new at the start of Simon's briefing. 'Gypo join in the turn into Diamond. There's no rush; take it easy.'

For many years the front five aircraft have been nick-named Enid, allegedly after Enid Blyton's Famous Five. For reasons which are lost in the mists of time, the rear four aircraft are usually known as Gypo, pronounced 'jippo'. A display take off is more demanding than it might seem. The aircraft line up on the runway in three groups: a three, a two, and a four, each group separated from the other by 750 feet. All aircraft release brakes at the same time on the command of the Leader. The middle group, Reds 4 and 5, use slightly more power than the leading group and actually get airborne a few seconds before Reds 1, 2 and 3. Because they are accelerating slightly faster than the leading group, Reds 4 and 5 quickly catch up and assume their accustomed position on the starboard and port wings respectively.

Once airborne, Gypo section changes into a box or mini-diamond formation, 6 in the lead, 7 directly astern and 8 and 9 in close formation on the right and left. Red 6 now has the tricky job of leading his section into position directly astern of Enid so that the nine aircraft merge in a perfect diamond as they all execute a steep climbing turn to the right. If Gypo Leader has too much of an overtake speed, he will have to fly his section either to one

In loose transit formation the
Team descend from high
altitude down into the valleys
and mountains of Switzerland,
en route to Sion.

Reds and Blues 1997. Reds from the left are: Mike Williams (10), Richie Matthews (8), Andy Offer (4), Tim Couston (6), Ian Smith (2), Simon Meade (1), Gary Waterfall (3), Andy Cubin (5), Dave Stobie (7), Sean Perrett (9) and Jon Russell (Jengo).
Blues from the left are: Dave Jones, Andy Nott, Mick Corden, Rich Penney, Brent Hall, Steve Reece, Andy Woods, Aidy Mills and Dave Webster.

side of the leading group or underneath them. Either way it will look unprofessional to the crowd below. If he has insufficient overtake speed, the complete diamond will probably not be formed until all the aircraft are out of sight behind the crowd. That would also be unprofessional and disappointing for the crowd. Either eventuality would lead to considerable banter at the debriefing.

Escape manoeuvres, both on the ground and in the air, had been discussed at some length at the pre-flight briefing. With all nine aircraft accelerating along the runway at the same time, it is essential that every pilot knows exactly what to do if one or more aircraft ahead of him abandons take off for any reason. This is even more demonstrative than the pilots, they did not show it – at least not in front of the pilots. Most of those working inside the hangar came outside to watch the take off, something they would never do for a normal departure. They stood around in small groups as though they had nothing better to do at that particular time, nonchalantly

The display site at Sion lies in a valley bracketed by mountains, requiring a modified display. Deep in thought, the Boss takes time on his own to mentally run through the revised sequence.

important when taking off from a runway such as Cranwell's, which is considerably narrower and shorter than Scampton's. In the air, every pilot has to bear in mind that there is no room for error.

The ground crew had worked hard until late in the night to get nine aircraft ready to fly. They, too, were excited about the first nine-ship formation but, being less

talking about anything but the first nine-ship. Everyone knew about the bet. Dave Chowns had made it clear that he would use his winnings to buy beer for the ground

As show time approaches, the Reds gather around 5's jet for the ritual briefing. But, with the modified display today, it's most certainly not just a formality.

crew but that was not the reason for their suppressed excitement.

As the nine aircraft lined up on runway 27, almost out of sight at the far end of the airfield, the clouds rolled back and the airfield was suddenly bathed in warm sunlight. The take off was without incident. Gypo joined up smoothly with Enid before the formation had completed 90 degrees of the turn – just perfect. A couple of minutes

later the formation made one pass, complete with 'whoosh', over Cranwell in Diamond Nine before disappearing from sight en route to Scampton. The clouds then reformed to blot out the sun – quite uncanny timing. There was a sense of disappointment as the noise of the nine jets receded. In every previous year, ground crew, familes and friends had been able to watch the full nine-ship practice but now there was a 30 minute gap while the aircraft operated over Scampton. BBC Radio Lincolnshire, maintaining their claim to be first in the county with the news, told their listeners about the first nine ship while the aircraft were still in action.

On the walk back to the Flight Line Control after

The Spanish team stop to watch in awe as Timmy and Stobes spin their Synchro magic. With a view angle to the side rather than on datum, the 'fudge' or actual distance between the two jets can clearly be determined.

landing, the pilots formally shook hands and congratulated each other in typical British gentlemanly fashion. Simon paused to say a special thank you to the ground crew, a nice touch, much appreciated. The crew room lunch that day was more refined than normal thanks to the generosity of John Cooper, a long-time friend of the Team. John, always known simply as 'Coops' to generations of Red Arrows, had astonished the motor-cycling fraternity in 1971 when, as a complete unknown and riding a 750cc bike borrowed from BSA, he defied all the odds and beat reigning world champion Giacomo Agostini in the Race of the Year at Mallory Park. Coops now runs his own motor and motor cycle business in Derby. He visits the Red Arrows at least once every year

(Above) The sun glints on the highly polished wings of the jets as they make a pass in Viggen formation, named after the Swedish air defence fighter.

(Left) With red smoke recording his path, Stobes winds his Hawk around Reds 6, 8 and 9 in Corkscrew, the manoeuvre appearing even more spectacular thanks to the dramatic backdrop.

and always comes with a vast hamper of cooked sausages, hams, black puddings, haslet, crispy bread, and cream cakes. Perhaps, sometime in the distant past, he had experienced one of the normal Red Arrows' lunches! On this occasion he travelled to Cranwell in his 20 year old, immaculately maintained, E-type Jaguar and

the pilots seemed to take more interest in that than in the briefing for their next sortie.

'I'm glad that's over,' said Gary Waterfall after the third nine-ship sortie of the day. Had he found the flying more difficult than he had expected? 'No, but it was *as* difficult as I'd expected. Of course, I'd flown four-ship formations many times before – all fast jet pilots do that as a matter of course – but I'd never looped and barrel rolled in formation. There were a lot of things I had to get used to. First, there was the seat – just like Andy Cubin, I had to find a seat position that was comfortable. Then, once I'd found the best position for me, it was important that I always put the seat in that same position otherwise all my references would be wrong. It took a few weeks getting used to that and to watching the Leader rather than watching the scenery. As a solo display pilot I'd had to watch the ground for most of my display – now I hardly ever get time to see the ground except when landing. We had to get used to acting precisely on the word of command from the Boss and we had to get used to the way he gave the orders. In the front line it's more a case of follow my leader but that doesn't work with precision formation aerobatics.

'I was surprised how tired, both physically and mentally, I got. At the end of the first month we had all flown about 50 formation sorties and we were absolutely shattered. I've found the other pilots a great help. They are always willing to give the benefit of their experiences if you are prepared to listen and learn. Sean, who flies in the 9 slot right behind me, has been particularly helpful – but he has a vested interest in ensuring that I do things properly!'

The following week, the last week before Spring Leave, was full of incident.

The most famous Red Arrows formation of all is Diamond Nine, the nine red jets displaying a perfect example as they thrill the Swiss with their mastery of the skies.

OSPs

'One of the main reasons for OSPs – out-of-season practices – is to give the ground support party an opportunity to practice their procedures,' explained Jon Russell on Monday 17 March. 'The idea is to fly off to an airfield away from base, with the Circus in the back seats, and then fly a full practice as though it was a proper public display. This gives the ground crew a chance to practice the planning and deployment procedures. Today we're doing an OSP at Linton-on-Ouse and we'll be making it a night stop.'

RAF Linton-on-Ouse is the Tucano basic flying training school near York. With so many young pilots and their instructors on base, the Red Arrows are assured of a highly critical audience and a lengthier than usual debriefing in the Officers' Mess bar afterwards. 'Away Days', however, have a still more important purpose. For the past five months the pilots had been practising over Scampton. The Team Leader and the four Gypo pilots had become so completely familiar with all the turning points and ground features that they had little need to concentrate on navigation and timing. During the display season this will all change. The pilots will often display at locations they have never seen before and so every transit and display sortie will have to be planned in great detail. OSPs can be a great way to check out and refine the planning procedures.

'Today the Circus will fly in the back seats for the transit flight to Linton,' continued Jon. 'However, because of the poor serviceability recently, the Boss needs to fly another practice out of Linton tomorrow morning before landing back at Cranwell. The back-seaters are not allowed to fly on displays or practice displays, so we're deploying a ground support party to Linton by road as well.'

It was the start of another busy and frustrating week. Andy Cubin had to travel to London on the

After an immaculate display, there's time to relax a little and enjoy the hospitality, but don't worry, Timmy, no one would dare steal your crisps! Actually Red 6 is not that fat – it's just a trick of the camera.

Tuesday to receive his MBE from the Queen, so once again Simon could not fly nine. On the following day the Red Arrows were scheduled to make a flypast over the

National Exhibition Centre at Birmingham for the official opening of an exhibition called Year of Engineering Success. BBC Television's *Tomorrow's World* programme, broadcasting live from the NEC at various times, intended to film the flypast. There were only six serviceable aircraft in Red Arrows' livery and because Simon was not willing to allow the Team to appear on national TV in borrowed aircraft, he flew just the six. The BBC wanted some dynamic air-to-ground footage of the Hawks flying over Birmingham to supplement the static coverage they would get from ground- based cameras at the NEC. To this end, a digital television camera was delivered to Cranwell so that one of the spare pilots could use it to take pictures from the back seat of one of the Hawks.

Occasionally, the Red Arrows are authorised to fly professional photographers and TV cameramen. They do

Au revoir and auf wiedersehen, Sion, it's time to slip those surly bonds once again and continue with the Team's hectic display schedule. Hold on to your hats, Cottesmore, here we come!

not like doing so on important occasions because if the cameraman is airsick it is likely that there will be no pictures at all. It is one thing flying as a passenger but it is quite a different matter having to peer continuously through a tiny viewfinder at a rapidly gyrating world whilst strapped tightly into an ejection seat and trying to remember from the pre-flight briefing all the drills that have to be carried out in the event of some dire in-flight emergency. Even handling the camera when gravity is changing from a negative figure to as much as plus 7 requires a major effort. Many photographers have taken pictures of their knee caps, or the inside of the cockpit, when their arms could no longer hold the camera up to their eyes as the force of gravity increased. Sorties have been cancelled in the past when the passenger became too ill to continue or dropped some of his equipment onto the cockpit floor where it might have jammed the flying controls. Modern miniature TV cameras are quite easy to use; focus and exposure are automatic so all the pilot in the back seat has to do is 'point and shoot' – although professional cameramen might not agree!

After landing, the cassette from the TV camera was handed to the waiting despatch rider and rushed immediately to the TV studio for editing. The Red Arrows' appearance on *Tomorrow's World* that evening lasted precisely 20 seconds, half of which was footage taken by the on-board camera. If only the viewers knew how much time and effort went into producing those few seconds of film.

There were corporate visitors on every day that week, as well as visits by students from the RAF's School of Aviation Medicine, and photo-shoots with three different, expensive sports cars. Judy Leedon, the holder of the world altitude hang-gliding record called in on

Moments after leaving Sion, the Reds join up in Diamond Nine – it would be a shame to miss the opportunity of a photograph with such spectacular mountain scenery.

(Left) 35,000 feet up in the deep blue yonder, there's no need for a smoke system as Mother Nature thoughtfully provides her own. Red 5, Andy Cubin, leaves a con trail in his wake as he clocks up his 4,000th flying hour – nearly all of which have been in fast jets.

A fish-eye lens view from the Mange's jet as he tucks in behind the Boss as the Red Arrows join up for their customary and spectacular loop and break into the Cottesmore circuit.

Wednesday with a group of her sponsors. Judy, who hang-glides from greater altitudes than the Red Arrows fly, had brought some superb high altitude photographs to show the pilots. There was so much going on that it was not easy for the pilots to get down to any planning for the forthcoming Cyprus detachment. 'It's very difficult trying to run a five-star restaurant in a crew room and do all my other jobs as well,' moaned Ian Smith, ducking hastily to avoid a plain digestive biscuit heading his way.

One seemingly innocuous visit to the Squadron that

Nice hat, Mange! Once on the ground, Mike Williams takes a rare opportunity to relax for a few minutes. The Manager's job is a demanding one, with many of the logistical and organisational problems, as well as the on-site PR, falling to him.

week was to have totally unforeseen repercussions some weeks later. Two senior officers from HM Customs and Excise at East Midlands Airport visited the Red Arrows to set up a 'Memorandum of Arrangement' whereby Cranwell could be used as an authorised port for UK entry and exit. A similar arrangement had been in force for many years at Scampton. The arrangement allows Customs officers to come to Cranwell so that the Red Arrows can comply with immigration and customs formalities at their home base when returning from overseas. This procedure saves a great deal of time and avoids the Hawks and any accompanying Hercules support aircraft having to make expensive and inconvenient landings at a UK Customs airfield before finally returning to base. After the Memorandum had been agreed, the pilots posed for a series of pictures with the Customs officials so that the story could be reported in *Portcullis*, HM Customs and Excise's in-house magazine. A few days later, after the Team had departed for Cyprus, the Customs officials returned to Cranwell for the formal signing of the memorandum by the Station Commander.

Four weeks later, while the Team was still on detachment to Cyprus, three national newspapers, on three consecutive days, rang the Team's PR officer and the Ministry of Defence Press Office asking for details of an alleged smuggling incident involving the Red Arrows. It seems a local freelance reporter had seen, or been told about, the Customs Officers' two visits to Cranwell and the meetings with the Red Arrows and later with the Station Commander, and had jumped to the conclusion that they must have been investigating a case of smuggling! There is always someone, somewhere, willing to write a knocking story about the Red Arrows. Fortunately, each of the newspapers concerned checked the story, found there was no truth in it, and so nothing was published.

In a typical year, the Team expects to fly about half a dozen OSPs before leaving for the annual detachment to Cyprus, but 1997 was not a typical year. The only other OSP flown was at Kirton Lindsey, about ten miles north of Scampton, a former RAF aerodrome now an Army base. The Circus could not be involved because the sortie started and finished at Cranwell.

'This OSP at Kirton is probably the most difficult display we'll fly all year,' said Simon at the pre-flight briefing. 'It's an old World War II grass airfield. There's nothing to mark the display line, but there are several large towers, hangars and other obstructions for Synchro to take note of. There are no services on the ground other than the Manager with his two-way radio. The nearest runways we can use in an emergency are Scampton to the south and Humberside airport to the north east. Mange will call me on his mobile as soon as he gets there to tell me the wind, visibility and the QFE.'

The QFE is the atmospheric pressure in millibars which, when set on the aircraft altimeter, will cause the altimeter to read zero feet at ground level on the airfield. The Leader and the Synchro pilots need an accurate QFE in order to know exactly how high they are above the ground. At active airfields the QFE is provided by the Duty Met Officer. At Kirton Lindsey the Manager, having driven by road from Cranwell, will find the QFE empirically by standing at Display Datum with a portable altimeter, turning a control knob until the needles indicate zero feet and then reading off the setting in millibars.

So much for the theory! Unfortunately, when Mike Williams tried to adjust the altimeter, the knob refused to move the needles. He tried to call the Met Officer on the mobile phone to obtain the latest QFEs for nearby airfields from which he could have interpolated a reasonably accurate figure for Kirton, but the phone refused to function. A quick dash over to the nearest Army office in one of the hangars to use one of their phones proved fruitless: the local telephone exchange was closed for servicing and all telephones were out of action.

By this time the Red Arrows were getting airborne from Cranwell wondering what had happened to the Manager. Several hundred spectators, including Army families from the base and teachers and their children

The Red Arrows employ some 80 ground support personnel. All are hard working and dedicated, but none more so than Corporal Spike Robertson, whose responsibility it is to maintain and fit all the flight kit.

from local schools, were gathering at Display Datum where boxes full of Red Arrows' brochures and stickers were opened and the contents distributed into eager hands. Mike eventually made two-way contact with Red Leader on a hand-held radio when the aircraft were about ten miles from Kirton Lindsey. He passed the weather details together with an estimated QFE worked out from first principles using his knowledge of the prevailing met conditions. Right on time the Red Arrows

whooshed overhead to the delight of the crowd.

The difficulties imposed by the site are the main reason for flying an OSP overhead Kirton Lindsey each year and many useful lessons were learned on this occasion. That was the final sortie of the winter training season. On the Friday evening the Team's officers and ladies were entertained to dinner by the Shell Oil Company at the Belton Woods Country Club near Grantham, a favourite haunt of the Team, and then everyone dispersed for nine days' leave.

The Circus never did get an opportunity to practice their procedures. The first time they flew in the back seats was on the first leg of the flight to Cyprus – and that was operational not practice.

(Pages 108-9) Microphone lowered, Mike allows the Cottesmore crowds to enjoy the dramatic Synchro Opposition Loop in silence. The smoke tendrals hanging in the sky are all that remain of the previous manoeuvre, the seven jet Vertical Split.

As Red 9 climbs up to join Buzz in the office, Dave 'Webbo' Webster responds to the parting levity. A bond of trust exists between the pilots and the Circus engineers and, although the job is taken very seriously, there's always time for some light-hearted banter between the Reds and the Blues.

The First Half

'The secret of getting to a display bang on time really starts all the way back in the planning room,' said Simon, describing the way he flies a typical display. 'If the guys haven't planned the sortie accurately enough, then it's a bit of a nightmare for me to get it right on the day. I aim to start the take-off run at the departure airfield to the nearest second and then I fly the plan as laid down on the map. All I have to do is to maintain exactly 360 knots ground speed. It's as simple as that and we should arrive, from crowd rear, over Display Datum within two seconds of the advertised time – just as the Manager gets to the bit where he says, "Would you please welcome the 1997 Royal Air Force Aerobatic Team, the Red Arrows!" It's a spectacular arrival although I say so myself.'

The days of the crowd rear arrival, which the Red Arrows have employed for most of the Team's life, might be numbered. Generally, no display aircraft is allowed to fly over the crowd. However, when the Red Arrows are in a stable formation and are at least 1,000 feet above the ground, as they are for the crowd rear arrival, or when they are approaching the crowd but diverging and climbing, as in the Vixen Break, the Team has a waiver to over-fly the crowd.

'The French and Dutch won't accept the waiver and that's why we don't fly in those two countries,' said Simon, answering a frequently asked question. 'The

It is 14 June, the Queen's birthday. The morning's pagentry and events are over and, as the Royal Family stand unseen beneath the camera point, the Red Arrows fly down the Mall to close the show. Few noticed at the time that there were only eight jets in the formation, not nine. Earlier that week, Red 3, Gary Waterfall (by now Squadron Leader Waterfall) had fallen while climbing into his jet, injuring his leg badly. It would be some time before poor old Gazzer would be fit to fly again.

Back at Cranwell HQ, Sean and Offo plot the course for the forthcoming Fairford and Lowestoft push. Transit timing and route selection are critical and, with ten jets in tow, an error in either could be, to say the least, rather embarrassing for the ambassadors of the RAF.

(Right) Red Leader tucks the wheels into the wells. Outboard of him, unseen, are Reds 2 and 3, and behind, partially hidden in the exhaust haze, are Reds 4 to 9.

waiver doesn't arise in the case of Germany because formation aerobatics have been banned there since the Frecce Tricolori had their accident at Ramstein in 1988.'

Simon has already considered how a withdrawal of the waiver would affect the display in case it happens during his tour of duty as Team Leader. 'I think it'll be a great shame if we do have to change to a crowd front show – but I can see it coming before my tour's over. The

way we arrive from crowd rear is perfectly safe and it's what I would call a proper arrival, with the Manager's introduction leading straight into that very satisfying whoosh. The Red Arrows have always done it that way. Having to start from either end of the display line would mean that the crowd could see us coming, from the left or right, for quite a long time and that would completely spoil the impact.'

For much of a display the Team Leader and, in the second half, Synchro Leader, have to fly at very accurate speeds. At low level there are two speeds to be considered: indicated air speed (IAS) and ground speed. IAS, which is directly related to the amount of lift being generated by the wings, is important for manoeuvres; there are minimum speeds for starting loops and barrel rolls and minimum safe speeds at the top of loops. Ground speed, which is the IAS corrected for wind, is all-important for time-keeping. The cockpit air speed indicator, as its name implies, reads IAS but there is no direct reading of ground speed from the standard pressure instruments. However, the Team Leader has a GPS satellite receiver which he can set up to display an accurate ground speed.

'Depending on the actual wind on the day, for the final run in to the site I adjust the IAS to achieve my desired ground speed. With about a minute to go, when I've positively identified a particular landmark, I swap from the small-scale chart I've used up till then, to a large-scale Ordnance Survey map. After that it's a case of thumbing – that's nudging my thumb along the track line on the map – to get precisely over the Datum. We're going quite fast – 360 knots is about 420 statute mph, that's seven miles a minute, so my thumb moves down the map quite quickly! That last minute is one of the trickiest parts of the show for me; I have a lot of decisions to make. First of all, I've got to get the guys out into

The jets spread out for another high altitude transit, keeping them out of the way of light aircraft, microlytes, hang-gliders, balloons and birds!

"Big Nine" ready for the arrival loop.'

Big Nine is a very wide formation, four aircraft in echelon on either side of the Leader. Adjusting the formation's heading by just a couple of degrees in that configuration, in an attempt to move 200 metres to the left or right, would make life very difficult for all eight pilots, but especially for the two furthest from the Leader.

'In the last 30 seconds, because we're then so close to Display Datum, I'll accept any slight errors in track or timing in the interests of having a stable formation. I have my first proper look at the weather at the site and I talk to the Mange to update the QFE and to hear about any extra hazards he might have seen. If there's any cloud around, I need to decide whether there's a gap large enough for us to loop in. If I haven't got enough clear sky for the pull up into the Diamond Nine arrival loop, I'll stay in Nine Arrow, three either side of me with 6 and 7 in line astern, and go instead into the rolling display.

'Then I stow my maps away – I don't need them any more. If I'm committed to a looping arrival, I check that I have sufficient speed. 360 knots IAS is the absolute minimum but I try to have an extra 20 knots or so to give Dave Stobie in the 7 slot a bit more thrust to play with. We pull up at $3^{1}/2$ g. In the first half of the loop we change into Diamond Nine, our trademark formation, and the speed bleeds quickly away as we climb. Stobes needs the most energy because he has to decelerate slightly from his Big Nine position out on the wing and then accelerate into his next position right at the back of the Diamond. If it's a hot day, when the engine gives less thrust, or if I have too few knots when I start the pull, it's Dave who suffers. The crowd would blame him for being slow into position but really it would be my fault. We go

Red 5 pulls it in close to 4, giving us a rather spectacular view of the underside. The centreline smoke pod is actually a modified gun pod, designed to carry a 30-mm Aden cannon.

As the formation approaches Fairford, they will join up in Big Nine for the spectacular Arrival Loop – cloud base permitting. If not, it'll be a run and break.

For any aerobatic team a powerful and effective smoke system is vital, both to make the small aircraft stand out against the sky and to add shape and creativity to the display.

over the top at 150 knots about 5,500 feet above the ground – that's just over a mile high.

'I fly the loop as accurately as I can, because the slightest angle of bank causes quite a large twist. When I come over the top, I look back over my head to check our position relative to the smoke trails we made on the way up. If I've flown a perfectly straight loop and I come down to the left or right of the trails, that gives me an accurate indication of the wind vector. Speed rapidly increases as we near the bottom of the loop. I pull hard left and position for a Diamond Bend down the line past the crowd at 300 feet. As we pass Datum, I check along the line of the display visually to make sure there are no unexpected hazards.'

The formation changes from Diamond to Short Diamond, a tighter version of the same thing. This small adjustment makes the next change, into EFA, a lot easier and more pleasing on the eye. EFA is the Red Arrows' representation of the European Fighter Aircraft. To achieve this, the

(Above) There's no point in getting too tense about this display flying business, as Red Leader and Synchro Leader demonstrate. Originally Simon served with the Team from 1991 to 1993, himself flying in the Red 6 Synchro Leader position in his final year. Indeed, most leaders of the Red Arrows have been ex-Synchro pilots.

(Right) High above Fairford in Gloucestershire, Reds 1, 2, 4 and 5 loop in Caterpillar, the more familiar five-ship manoeuvre being reduced by Gary Waterfall's absence.

outside aircraft slide backwards whilst the stem, Reds 1, 6 and 7, maintain their position. It is vital that the Leader maintains his angle of bank while this is going on because the four aircraft that are moving backwards might not pick up any sideways oscillation in the stem and that could result in a close encounter – or even one aircraft clipping the wing of another. EFA stretches a long way back and the rearmost aircraft go out of the Leader's vision in his rear-view mirror.

Reds 2 to 5 follow the Boss in Leader's Benefit.

'So that I know when it's safe for me to start manoeuvring again, I delegate to Red 4 the "Smoke Off" call – he's well placed right at the back to see all the aircraft clearly. When he calls "Smoke off", I know it's safe to make whatever manoeuvres I need. If there's been a problem in the change, Red 4 will not make that call and I'll then maintain whatever angle of bank I have on and wait until the problem has been resolved – even if that means flying away from the crowd.'

That rule applies to every change; if someone does not make an expected radio call, then no one changes position.

'Incidentally,' continued Simon, with the air of someone imparting privileged information, 'the Red Arrows always barrel roll to the left. Not a lot of people know that! If we routinely did some rolls to the left and some to the right, it would need just one pilot to roll the wrong way for any reason and we would get into an awful mess. Every pilot knows that all the rolls are to the left – we've practised them that way all winter so we're mentally attuned.

'There is an anecdote,' he added, with a wistful smile, 'that a Leader once screwed up his position relative

to the Datum and blandly announced on the radio that the next barrel roll would be to the right in order to regain position. The story goes that the Leader was thoroughly debriefed by the rest of the Team on his change of plan soon after landing! It would've been nice to have been the proverbial fly on the wall at that debriefing. Of course, we could include both left- and right-hand rolls in the programme but, since the vast majority of the public would not notice, it makes sense to keep things simple and safe.'

Because positive g is applied throughout barrel rolls, the entire formation moves slightly sideways during the rolls, even when there is no wind. 'We travel about two miles along the crowd line during a barrel roll

Gypo head in towards datum and the crowd, rolling in preparation for the spectacular Gypo Break.

and in that distance we can traverse sideways quite a significant amount – the actual distance depends on the wind. I have to be particularly careful not to infringe the display line, that's a safety line parallel to and in front of the crowd. Any pilot crossing the display line will incur the wrath of the display supervisor.'

There are two radios in each aircraft. One is a VHF set used mainly for air-to-ground communications. The other is a UHF set used solely for internal formation

Precise and meticulous logs are kept of all flying hours and stress loading to the air frames. Jon Russell, the junior engineer, or Jengo, methodically enters the relevant information on the Flying Log and Fatigue Data Sheet.

comms. The Manager transmits some of the pilots' chat over the PA system during his commentary so that everyone in the crowd can get a flavour of what goes on.

'Why do we seem to shout a lot on the radio? Mostly it's pure theatrics – particularly during those bits when we know the Manager is re-transmitting the calls over the PA system. But, I can convey extra information sim-ply by my intonation. For example, if I put a lot of aggression in my "pulling up" call, the guys know that I'm going to pull straight to 4g and they're ready for it. Another call is "Tight'ning" – I use that to indicate that I'm about to increase the g load. I put a lot of force into the second syllable if I am going to increase g aggressively and by a large amount.

'For accurate positioning, I might need to reduce the g loading to slacken a turn. The call is "Letting it out" and the guys have to know which bit of my transmission is the executive command. If I "let it out" without warning, some of the pilots would find themselves looking right into the jet pipe of the aircraft in front. The engine doesn't like being fed with the turbulent jet efflux which is at about 600 degrees. It's dangerous and could lead to an engine malfunction.

'The pilots can never wait until they see my aircraft start to move, they will always be late. Nor can they anticipate – that could be even more dangerous. We all have to make our control inputs at exactly the same instant. To start a loop the order is "And pulling up". I can drawl the "and" as long as necessary but I apply the control input on the "p" of pulling. Entering a barrel roll the order is "Pulling up and rolling". I start applying back pressure on the "p" of pulling and start applying aileron input on the "r" of rolling. In each case the "and" is the precursor to the executive and I stress that word strongly.'

A new manoeuvre introduced by Simon is a quarter clover leaf. It is flown in Apollo, the Red Arrows' representation of the American space rocket. Apollo is the tightest of all the formations; individual aircraft are just eight to ten feet apart. A full clover leaf is an academic aerobatic manoeuvre taught to student pilots as a precision exercise. It consists of four consecutive loops with a ninety degree bend at the top of each so that the aircraft eventually finishes up pointing in the same direction as when it started – hopefully.

'The quarter clover we do is one loop with a ninety degree twist at the top.' Simon demonstrates by use of his hands. 'It's a great way of changing direction to stay close to the crowd. This is the one manoeuvre that I can't afford to take into cloud because at the top we're both looping and rolling. It would be very disorientating for everyone if we went into cloud at that crucial point. As far as I know, this is the first time the Red Arrows have done a clover leaf. In the past it had always been deemed too difficult, especially for the guys out on the wing. The bit of the display the guys like least is coming down from the quarter clover and screwing to the left to convert into the horizontal plane. It's the most difficult part of the display to fly – especially if the wind is from crowd left, which means I have to turn even earlier.'

Ear protection is vital when working extensively in close proximity to jet aircraft, otherwise permanent hearing loss can result.

Flanker, the NATO name for the Sukhoi SU-27 fighter bomber as flown by the Russian Knights, is next, a new shape for 1997. 'We meet Russian display pilots regularly so we thought we'd put in a shape representing one of their best display aircraft. Getting into Flanker is a difficult and complex change because while Reds 4 and 5 are moving forwards from the back of Apollo, Reds 2 and 3 are moving backwards from the front and they all meet in line abreast in the middle. After the Flanker Bend we change into Fred, that's our abbreviation for Feathered Arrow, and I end the first half with a five-four split which gets us nicely into two groups in front of the crowd. The choreography of the second half is much more complicated. The Synchro manoeuvres and the main section manoeuvres have to be perfectly coordinated so that they flow nicely one after the other without any gaps and without any overlaps. I'll let Synchro Leader describe the second half.'

Bad Smell Hold

'The five-four split is the start of the second half,' said Tim Couston, Synchro Leader. 'That's my first real opportunity to back off, take a good look around and assess the site. We're into two sections now. The speed is around 350 knots. I turn to be slightly behind the Boss but paralleling his track and I just mirror his manoeuvres. It's quite a gentle manoeuvre from Gypo's point of view – it's only about 2g. As he turns in, I try to roll in at the same rate, same speed. I'm looking to pass quite close behind and slightly high on the Boss, normally through the left wingman's smoke to make the fudge look right for the crowd.'

At the Crunchie party, Lieutenant-Colonel Pier Luigi Fiore, Commander of the Frecce Tricolori, presents Simon with a customised bottle of champagne to mark the event. A close camaraderie exists between the Reds and their genial Italian counterparts.

(Opposite)During the Fairford weekend, the Crunchie Flying Circus Wingwalking Team arranged a very exclusive party, just for them, the Red Arrows and the Italian display team, the Frecce Tricolori. An additional bonus for anyone present was the chance to see the Boss doing a spot of daredevil barnstorming atop the wing of a Stearman biplane.

Tim talks a lot about fudges, the little cheats put into Synchro's patterns to make it look as though the two soloists are meeting exactly head on. The fact that a great

Off the east coast at Lowestoft, Timmy and Stobes complete a perfect Heart, always a favourite with the public. Unfortunately on this occasion the crowd was reduced due to poor weather, but at least the Team was able to fly.

deal of thought and skill goes into the fudges emphasises the sheer professionalism of the Red Arrows' display. The Synchro Pair spend quite a lot of time crowd rear, theoretically out of sight of the crowd while the main section do their stuff on centre stage, but even crowd rear all the movements are carefully worked out and timed.

'When the five-four split is complete, we reverse our turn to go behind the crowd – out of sight. While the main section is performing in front of the crowd, I do a tear-drop timing pattern to bring Gypo around from right to left to set up for the Corkscrew. I watch the Boss as he's finishing his manoeuvre and then I time my turn on to the display line so that we're ready to go as soon as the main section's finished. For the Corkscrew we fly at 330 knots, 300 feet above the ground so that there's plenty of room underneath for Red 7 to do his revolving. Reds 8 and 9 are on the wing. Stobes starts the manoeuvre by calling "Smoke on go" and "aboard". He then does three barrelling revolutions around the three of us, anticlockwise. Once he gets to the top of his first upswing, I call 8 and 9 to roll inverted. They do that together while I stay upright. When they're happy and steady, they call "Clear" and then "go" in turn. On the "Go", I roll inverted to the right and they roll out to the right, back to the upright position. The idea is that the wings of the three aircraft should stay parallel as we roll. By this time, Stobes is completing his third barrel roll around us and re-forms line astern on me, he calls "Complete" and I roll to the upright position. I call "Smoke off go" and that's our first manoeuvre complete.'

The main section then fly the Twizzle, a graceful falling-leaf manoeuvre, from crowd right to crowd left.

'While the Twizzle is going on, Gypo stays crowd front getting into position for the Gypo Break. A quick burst on the tone from me tells the guys to go the starting position, and then we intercept the line 90 degrees to the Datum. I aim for 350 knots – it's quite a fast manoeuvre. The Boss finishes the Twizzle with a "smoke off go" call, then I give our "smoke on" call as soon as we're stabilised pointing directly at the crowd. The next call is "Gypo roll go". Red 6 and 7 pitch and roll away from the centre of the turn, through a whole revolution and a bit, then pull towards each other and cross. There's lots of length in the formation although it's designed to look from the crowd's viewpoint as if there are four aircraft line abreast. If you can see it from the side, you can see the distance between each aircraft in the formation. I fly

predictable parameters, 7 flies to avoid me slightly high to make the fudge look right to the crowd, then after the cross 8 and 9 fly to crowd rear, switch their smoke off and go into their holding pattern.'

The holding pattern flown crowd rear by Reds 8 and 9 has become known as the 'Bad Smell' hold – presumably suggesting why they have been cast off from the rest of the Team. Out crowd front, Reds 6 and 7 wing over at each end of the line then come around for the Double Rolls.

'The Double Rolls are flown at 300 knots, starting at 100 feet above the ground. On the executive "Pull – go" from me, we pitch to 20 degrees nose up and both roll to

The Red Arrows operated out of Exeter Airport for the Culdrose and Middle Wallop shows. But this time the weather was just too bad, the Team cancelling their display at Culdrose. It did give the Blues a chance for a breather.

the left. During this manoeuvre we actually cross sides between the first and second rolls. After the first complete roll we stabilise back at 100 feet above the ground. The second "Pull – go" is hopefully just before the cross at Display Datum. After the second roll we pitch and clear to the rear.

'When we get crowd rear we pick up 8 and 9 again

from their Bad Smell holding pattern and we all join up initially at 300 knots. The speed is quite critical because I have to turn through 270 degrees, pick up three other aircraft and arrive at the right speed for the next manoeuvre, the Card Loop. Red 7 flies line abreast on me and Red 8 and 9 fly line astern on their respective sides to make a square. I must accelerate to 350 knots before I can pull up into the loop. On the way down from the top of the loop, we split four ways and come down to low level again. Reds 8 and 9 go off to crowd right to re-join the main section, while 6 and 7 do another crowd front pattern with a wing over at each end.

'Our next manoeuvre is the Opposition Barrel Roll. I line up on the display line, 330 knots. We then feint a right turn towards each other, quickly reverse and execute a barrel roll to the left. For each of these crowd front manoeuvres we put the white smoke on at the end of the line which is about 3,000 feet from Datum. The smoke is partly to keep the crowd's eyes on us but it is also a visual aid for us – so that we can see each other. That's especially important when the visibility is not perfect.'

Synchro's next manoeuvre is either the Opposition Loop, when the cloud base is high enough, or the Carousel, which is essentially a horizontal loop.

'For the Op Loop Dave sets himself up slightly low on me and we run in at 350 knots. On my command "Pull – go" we both apply full power and pull to the buffet. We reach about 7g – we haven't time to look at the accelerometer and, in any case, we don't have to worry about the amount of g. We know we can't over-stress the aircraft by pulling too hard if we start at the correct

'Get off your horse and drink your milk' Smithy style. Not chaps for horse riding, but rather his as yet unfastened anti-g suit flapping in the wind.

(Right) Perfection is everything with the Red Arrows. Even the chocks that await the returning aircraft are set out with care and precision.

(Previous pages) In the moist evening skies over the Army Air Corps base at Middle Wallop, the multi-coloured smoking jets stand out dramatically against the white cloud, streamers of vapour spiralling off the jets' wing tips as they curve down in Twizzle formation.

(Left) A crescendo of music from the London Philharmonic Youth Orchestra punctuates a perfectly executed Vixen Break.

speed. Pulling to the buffet is the common denominator. Because each aircraft has a similar performance, if we both pull to the buffet, we'll both reach the top of the loop at the same height. As a matter of fact, Dave actually starts at 360 knots, ten more than me, because he flies a slightly larger loop than I do. He crosses outside of me on each of the crosses.

'The g decreases as the speed decreases but we stay on the buffet until 80 degrees nose up and after that we relax the back pressure gently. If we pulled on the buffet all the way round it would be a very weird looking loop – as the speed reduces the turn rate also reduces and so we need to round out the loop at the top. I'm looking for my gate height – I must reach the inverted position at the top at an absolute minimum of 4,000 feet above the ground, and less than 200 knots, in order to complete the loop safely. Actually, I try to float it at the top to 4,500 feet to have some room to play with to get the third cross sorted out. It's my responsibility to make sure both aircraft are at a safe height because Red 7 really doesn't have time to look in at his altimeter. On a really good cross I can hear 6's engine as we pass.

'If the cloud base is too low for the Op Loop, we go for the Carousel option. Both aircraft fly at 330 knots. Just before we cross directly in front of Datum, I call "turn" and we both roll to 80 degrees of bank and pull to $4\frac{1}{2}$ g. It looks such a simple manoeuvre but it's actually very difficult because we have to fly partly on instruments to get the necessary precision. It's essential that I maintain exactly $4\frac{1}{2}$ g and 330 knots and I've got to

Resembling ducklings following their mother, the Reds taxi back into Exeter in the evening light.

climb slightly so that as we get further away from the crowd it looks level to the spectators. Round the back, Dave's looking to get himself just outside my trajectory and slightly high on me – another fudge. Since each of us is flying at 330 knots, we have a closing speed of about 800 statute mph – quite dynamic! After the rear cross we both need to over-bank slightly beyond 90 degrees because we have to lose the height we gained in the first half of the carousel. I still have to fly accurately at 4½ g

and 330 knots and get the height down to 150 feet by about seven-eighths of the way round so that Dave can sort himself out on me for the third cross. There's quite a lot to think about.'

After the main section has flown the Roll backs, Synchro Pair prepare for the Shotgun, flown with the two aircraft very close together at 150 feet, 350 knots.

'The sequence is, "Smoke on" then "Seven, roll go". Dave rolls right to the inverted position, slightly on my right-hand side and very slightly lower than me. It has to look as though he is directly line astern of me, stepped down slightly. When he's happy Dave calls "Go" and then "Go" again. On each "go" we roll our aircraft

through 90 degrees while maintaining height. That results in Dave being upright and me upside-down. We do those 90 degree rolls by using a full right deflection on the ailerons and a kick of left rudder to prevent the nose from dropping.'

While the aircraft is flying with 90 degrees of bank, the wings are not generating any vertical lift and so the nose of the aircraft will start to drop towards the ground. By applying left rudder, the rudder surface generates a vertical component of lift sufficient to enable the aircraft to remain in level flight for a few seconds. When the aircraft is inverted, the control column has to be pushed forward to generate minus 1g in order to maintain level flight.

With engines shut down for the day, the pilots dismount from their cockpits, handing the jets over to the ground crew for them to secure for the night.

'When I'm happy with my inverted position I call "Clear" on the radio and Dave rolls to the inverted, line astern of me. When he's happy with his position he calls "In", then I start a further slight push on the control column to start the aircraft gently climbing before we both roll out to the erect position. We put smoke off as we complete the manoeuvre.'

The Shotgun is the most complicated of Synchro's

Flying back along the south coast from Exeter, destination Kleine Brogel in Belgium, the scarlet jets shine in the sun, contrasting beautifully with the azure sea.

manoeuvres but the crowd's favourite is the Heart.

'We pull up at 350 knots about a couple of kilometres in front of Datum, into the vertical and then split by rolling 90 degrees away from each other, We pause for a moment and then pull to the nibble – the light buffet – with full power applied. We keep the back pressure applied all the way over the top, with the smoke on, until we get to 40 degrees nose down. We hold the 40-degree angle until we cross – that make's the pointy bit at the bottom of the heart. We switch the smoke off just before we cross.'

How do they arrange to cross directly in front of Datum when there is a strong wind along the Display Line? Both aircraft drift downwind together so the pilots need to know what component of wind is blowing along the line. If there is a 30-knot component of wind blowing from left to right, the aircraft travelling from left to right will have an extra 30 knots of ground speed while the other one, flying into wind, will have his ground speed reduced by thirty knots.

'It's a question of geometry really. For every five knots of head wind, we extend in our respective directions for one second. In a strong wind we can be counting for quite a long time. We even take account of climbing angles. For example, if we pitch to 45 degrees nose up, we count one and a half times the wind; 30 degrees pitch up, we count once the wind; as we come off the top of the Heart we count only half the wind. So there's a different wind correction for every manoeuvre. We also employ the "feeling in the water" technique. If we see that the main section is running a few seconds late, we need to extend our crowd rear pattern accordingly so we don't arrive too early. We use what we call the "arb plus" technique – an arbitrary correction suggested by the feeling in the water! There isn't time to do any clever mathematical calculation.'

FFNGs, PDA and a New Baby

'Springhawk is all about team building – and when I say team, I include everyone,' explained Simon Meade. 'We've done the first nine-ship, we've flown a few OSPs, we've had a bit of leave and we're all feeling pretty pleased with ourselves. Now we have to put it all together, polish up the routine and get ready to appear in public. Cyprus is a good place to do it. We bring virtually the whole Squadron with us – not just for a spring holiday but because we do more concentrated flying here at Akrotiri than we do at home.'

Transiting across rural Belgium, the Team form up into Big Nine as, nearing Kleine Brogel, we look down on to Sean Perrett's jet. In his back seat sits Dave Webster, one of the nine Circus engineers, chosen for their various skills, who fly on the transit sorties.

The Red Arrows' first spring detachment to RAF Akrotiri was in 1980, although the name Springhawk seems not to have been used until 1986. The intention is to escape the vagaries of the English spring and take advantage of the usually fine and predictable Mediterranean weather – but this sometimes backfires. It did in April 1997. Whilst most of the United Kingdom basked in unseasonably hot weather, Cyprus was subjected to severe thunderstorms, strong winds and torrential rain. There was even a freak snowstorm at Dhekelia, a seaside resort not far from Akrotiri. However the weather did not delay the flying programme unduly.

In recent years, Springhawk has become the time when the FFNGs, the pilots short-listed for selection, join the current Team for flying tests, interviews and assessment of their social acceptability. There is probably no other squadron in the RAF where squadron members are allowed to choose their successors, but then the RAF Aerobatic Team is like no other squadron.

'Originally there were nine pilots on the short list,' explained Gary Waterfall, 'but one was removed almost as soon as he got into the list – the RAF decided they had another job for him. There will be three vacancies at the end of this year, so each had about a one-in-three chance of being selected. I knew exactly how the FFNGs felt because it seemed like only yesterday when I was one. It was a very odd experience for me being on the other side of the fence although the procedure was exactly as I'd expected. The very frank chats we had about each candidate made me wonder what was said about me last year! It's a pretty good selection system – but it's probably not foolproof. Naturally all the FFNGs are on their very best behaviour. Like anyone else going for a new job, they're out to create an impression and so they probably don't behave completely naturally. That has to be taken into account.

'I knew the Harrier pilots on the short list professionally. One of them, Andy Lewis, is the 1997 Hawk display pilot. Obviously he had a bit of a head start

A view forward from Andy Cubin's jet as we taxi in to park up on a spare runway at Kleine Brogel, the Reds' operating base for the Sanicole show.

because he was already demonstrating in public his skill as a Hawk pilot, but that in itself did not mean he would necessarily make a good team member. We did select him though. I knew of the other applicants but only really at second hand.

'First of all, each of the FFNGs has a pure flying test. Then the Boss sits down with us and tells us how the flying test went and we discuss each candidate in detail, putting in any personal knowledge we might have – and any hearsay. If one of us doesn't like a particular candidate, we say so and explain why. Because someone has got on to the short list and passed a flying test doesn't necessarily mean that he is suitable for the Team. It's quite possible for someone who is relatively unknown to get on the short list on the basis of his previous professional reports. It's only when you get to spend a whole week with someone that you really get to find out what he's like.'

The first and second year pilots can, if they feel strongly enough, blackball a candidate on the grounds that they feel they could not work with him. That privilege is not accorded to the third year pilots because they will not have to work with him.

'The professionalism, pure flying skill, of the candidate is taken for granted,' continued Gary. 'They should not have got this far if they're not capable of doing the flying to the required standard. In any case, we don't see the candidates doing their professional job during the selection week. You might be on your best behaviour at interview but you can't keep it up for a whole week – especially standing in the bar at half past eleven on a Friday night. It's vitally important to find out what they're like socially because you're going to be living with them for one, if not two years. In the heat of the display season, in the middle of August when you've been on the road together for maybe ten consecutive days, the last person you want on the Team is a loner, a complainer, or someone who is difficult to get on with, however good a flyer he might be.'

What happens if there is a disagreement?

'It usually seems to happen, so they tell me, that the short list gets reduced fairly quickly to about four

Mange supplies the informative dialogue as the Reds fly past the Sanicole control tower in Apollo formation. Earlier, the Team had been scheduled to display at Ostend, but the display there was cancelled due to a fatal crash the previous day.

and then instead of deciding who you're going to select, it's a question of which one you are not going to select. That can be the hardest part of it. If we can't agree straight away, then we go away and think about it, perhaps talk in small groups, before we get together again. Some years, apparently, the short list is very quickly reduced to three and then there's no further selection involved. I'm not going to say how it worked out this year because that would be unfair to the five we did not select.'

During their time in Cyprus, each of the short-listed pilots had an interview with the Simon Meade, the Commandant of CFS, Air Commodore Gavin Mackay, and his senior staff officer, Wing Commander Dick Johnston. No outsider has ever been allowed to sit in on the interviews. At the end of the week, the aspirants returned

The show's over and there's just time for a beer or two as Offo shares a joke with the ground crew.

home; they would hear their fate later. In the meantime, the 1997 Team continued polishing their display.

Before the Team is allowed to display in public, the Red Arrows' Commander-in-Chief has to grant Public Display Authority (PDA). This is, in effect, the Team's licence, renewable annually. When the Team Leader is satisfied that his display is safe and meets the high standards expected, he invites the C-in-C to watch.

Since 1989, PDA has been granted by the Commander-in-Chief at the end of the Springhawk detachment. Rather like the 'man from Del Monte' in the well-known advertisement, the C-in-C's approval cannot be taken for granted. The only occasion in recent years when he declined to award PDA at the first attempt was in 1991 when a display had to be aborted as a result of a clear air microburst, severe turbulence rolling off the nearby mountains. The nine aircraft scattered in all directions, which did at least give the pilots a rare opportunity for all nine of them to demonstrate their escape manoeuvres.

The day when the C-in-C gives PDA has, over the years, become known as Red Suit Day. At the end of the PDA sortie the Team Leader conducts a post-flight debriefing just as he does at the end of every sortie. When the debriefing is over, the Leader asks the C-in-C if he wishes to say anything. As soon as the C-in-C indicates that he will authorise the Team to display in public, off come the green flying suits the pilots have worn throughout the winter and on go the immaculate tailor-made red flying suits which just happen to be hanging ready close by. Thereafter, until the end of the season, the pilots will wear red suits.

'One of my more pleasant duties as Air Member for Personnel and the Team's Commander-in-Chief, is to come out to RAF Akrotiri to meet the Red Arrows,' said Air Marshal Sir David Cousins as he settled down to evaluate the performance. 'I have, of course, watched and admired the Team for many years but this is the first occasion I've had to watch them for strictly profes-

sional reasons. The granting of Public Display Authority is a serious business – no one knows that better than the Team Leader and his pilots. I'm looking to answer two questions: first, is the display up to the required high standard; and second, is it safe, both for the pilots and the spectators? I have to be satisfied on both counts.'

PDA was granted by the C-in-C on 1 May. The following day was a non-flying day, allowing the Team members to recover from the Red Suit Day celebrations. The first public day was on Saturday 3 May, at Akrotiri for an Open Day organised by the Soldiers, Sailors and Air Forces' Association (SSAFA). Immediately after landing, Red 3 quickly changed into civilian clothes and was driven to the civilian airport at Larnaca for a flight back to London on British Airways. A car was waiting at Heathrow in the early hours of Sunday morning to drive Gary back home and about 24 hours later his second child, Oliver, was born in Grantham Hospital. Little did he know at the time, but Gary would be doing a lot more babysitting than he had expected.

Gary's Hawk was flown back to England by Squadron Leader Andy Wyatt, a former Red Arrow now flying a desk at the Command Headquarters in Gloucester. He did not need much persuading to fly out to Cyprus to bring back a red jet.

Many visitors were hosted during Springhawk but perhaps the oddest encounter was with a retired British Army doctor whose hobby is collecting aircraft sick bags. He met the Team at Akrotiri and donated £25 to the Team's own charity for five RAF sick bags signed by the Red Arrows, thereby bringing his collection to almost 1,000.

During the 24 flying days in Cyprus the Team flew 57 formation practices. In addition, the Team Leader flew with all the FFNGs and each of the Red Arrows' pilots flew their annual sortie with the CFS Examiners. In all, from leaving Cranwell on 2 April until arriving back at base on 6 May, 647 aircraft sorties were flown, amounting to 396 flying hours.

Train Spotting

'How would you like a high-speed train named after the Red Arrows?' This question had come completely out of the blue one day in March in a telephone call to the PRO from Kelvin Bayldon, Account Manager for Virgin Trains. 'All our train sets are being repainted in a very striking red and dark grey livery.'

'I am sure we'd be delighted but there's already a train named after us,' the PRO replied. 'It's 91004, one of East Coast Main Line's Intercity 125s, and it was named by The Queen Mother at Kings Cross in 1989. I'm not sure whether we could have two trains named after us. It might seem greedy and it might confuse the spotters.'

But, as the Team were to learn, Kelvin is not easily put off. Two months later, 49 members of the Red Arrows, including all the Reds, a group of the Blues and a fair sprinkling of wives, partners and children, drove by coach to York and gathered in the Royal York Hotel for a VIP reception.

After an excellent lunch, everyone made their way through the railway station concourse to platform 10, where a gleaming train set was standing ready to form the 1407 scheduled service to Bristol Temple Meads.

Food is definitely the order of the day and, en route to the hotel, a stop at the local McDonald's fits the bill nicely.

Sadly, although the event had been widely advertised in advance, there were not many train-spotters on hand; perhaps they were kept at bay by the British Transport Police. After introductory remarks by Virgin Trains' Chief Executive, Brian Barrett, Simon Meade was invited to make a short speech and carry out the actual naming.

'You may not know this, but Richard Branson has been associated with the Red Arrows for a number of years. He flew a full display sortie with Tim Miller, one of my predecessors, seven years ago – and that is not an exploit to be undertaken lightly. I was there that day, just about to start my first year with the Team. Richard now has ten ex-Red Arrows flying as pilots for Virgin Atlantic, including the Team Leader he flew with in 1990. So Richard could, if he wished, form his own Red Arrows' Team – albeit with rather ageing pilots! I am not sure whether that represents good teamwork and leadership or just plain head-hunting. Brian, please tell Richard that if he is thinking of poaching any of my pilots to use them as drivers on Virgin Trains – I would be grateful if he would wait until the end of my tour.

'Next Saturday we will meet this train again, between Exeter and Teignmouth, on that spectacular stretch of line along the sea wall, when we hope to make a series of flypasts over the train to take photographs for the benefit of the local tourist boards – and for the sheer pleasure of doing it. We hope that you, Brian, will fly in my back seat to see your train from a different angle.'

After the brief ceremony, the Red Arrows joined the train for the journey south to Derby. Because it was a normal scheduled service, there were fare-paying customers on board – many of whom turned out to be train-spotters rather than genuine travellers. The Red Arrows passed through the train distributing brochures and stickers and chatting to the passengers. Fortunately, many of them appeared to be Red Arrows' fans and perhaps they assumed that the Team's presence in their flying suits was part of Virgin Trains' on-board entertainment. Certainly no one complained, possibly because everyone was invited to share the free champagne and canapés. No one, apart from the pilots, even batted an eyelid when the senior conductor, encouraged by the blue-suiters, announced over the public address system that Spot Firth, one of the Red Arrows' fuel bowser drivers, was driving the train. It was not true, of course, but the pilots looked worried for a few seconds. Several of the pilots and ground crew were, however, invited into the cab to see the 'cockpit', accompanied, as the rules required, by a senior inspector. The Red Arrows left the train at Derby and rejoined their coach for the journey home.

The date selected for the naming ceremony was one of the few days off the Team would get during the entire display season. The date for the flypast of the train was governed by the rules of all flypasts: they have to be timed so that they can be flown without incurring additional expense. As it happened, the Red Arrows had to be in Exeter on 17 May for a display at Plymouth and it was easy to build the flypast into the schedule. This news caused Kelvin Bayldon a crisis of conscience: it was the very day set for his wedding and having been the instigator of the train-naming, he did not wish to miss the flypasts.

'How am I going to tell Annie that we have to change the wedding date?' he asked rhetorically. In the end, he wisely drew back from any further consideration of that option and reluctantly accepted that his date in Weston-super-Mare would have to take priority. Although Annie had learned to love the Red Arrows following a couple of visits to Cranwell with Kelvin, there seemed little doubt that she would not wish to postpone her wedding on their account.

'Pity really. It would have made a nice story,' mused the PRO sadly.

On the Friday afternoon before the trip to Exeter, the Team gave a private display at Marham in Norfolk for the students of the Royal College of Defence Studies. While the nine display pilots flew back to Cranwell to debrief and refuel, Red 10, who had been giving the commentary at Marham, flew direct to Exeter. All the other Reds plus Wing Commander Dick Johnston arrived in the vicinity of Exeter to find a very active thunderstorm sitting over the airfield. Visibility was reduced to about two kilometres in torrential rain and the cloud base was only a few hundred feet above the ground. Simon split the formation into four groups of three and two aircraft. The leader of each group would fly an Instrument Landing System (ILS) pattern which would guide the aircraft down to Decision Height, 200 feet above the runway, from which point the pilots would complete a visual formation landing – if they could see the runway!

ILS patterns are flown at low speed so that when the runway is sighted, the aircraft is already in the landing configuration. If the pilot does not sight the runway until 200 feet, he has barely 20 seconds to assess the situation and put the aircraft on the ground. If he does not see the runway at Decision Height, he has to climb away to a safe height and either try again or divert to another airfield. Instrument circuits use up considerably more fuel than a standard high-speed run and break into a visual circuit. The fourth group, Red 9 and Red 11, found themselves only eight miles out from the airport, while the other aircraft were still in the process of landing and clearing the flooded runway. Sean and Dick were rapidly approaching their minimum safe fuel level, and, to further complicate matters, Dick's VHF radio was unserviceable which meant that he could not hear or talk to the air traffic controllers although he could communicate with Sean on the UHF military frequencies. Had any of the first eight aircraft blocked the runway for any reason, Reds 9 and 11 would have been stranded with nowhere to land. Sean prudently decided to carry out an emergency diversion to Cardiff airport while there was still sufficient fuel remaining.

Although Cardiff had been selected as the primary alternate airfield before leaving Cranwell, the incident does highlight the importance of meticulous pre-flight planning. Flying single-engined aircraft on minimum fuel in appalling conditions is no time to start getting out the planning documents! After refuelling at Cardiff, Reds 9 and 11 flew back to Exeter, by which time the weather had improved considerably.

The Blues arrived at the airport on the Saturday morning at about 9.30 am to start preparing the aircraft for the day's activities. Red Arrows' brochures and stickers, left in various places in the airport terminal, were snapped up by holiday-makers arriving from and just setting out for Tenerife, Palma and the Channel Islands. Some passengers, alighting from their holiday jet, made a beeline across the tarmac for the Hawks, much to the consternation of the airline movements staff who were trying to shepherd them into customs and immigration. The flight crew of a Lufthansa Regional Jet took time out to examine the Reds' Hawks at close quarters before re-boarding their own aircraft for a flight to Hamburg. A crowd of onlookers parked in every available lay-by on the narrow road that leads from the A30 to the airport.

Brian Barrett, having eaten a hearty breakfast, arrived shortly afterwards with his wife and daughters. He was quite keyed up but insisted that he was really looking forward to his flight. The weather, unfortunately, was still very poor. The overnight heavy rain and the moist southerly airstream produced a dew point of 20 degrees. Since the air temperature was also 20 degrees, that meant 100 per cent humidity and, inevitably, fog swirled around reducing visibility at times to less than one kilometre. Overhead, the sun occasionally poked through the overcast. The conditions were almost monsoon-like. Someone referred to it as 'hot fog', a very graphic but not very technical description. With just an hour to go before take-off, Simon had no option but to cancel the flypast.

No sooner had Simon announced his decision than the sun broke through the cloud and the air temperature climbed two or three degrees in as many minutes. This created a classic suckers' gap, named after

those foolish aviators who are sometimes tempted to ignore the weather forecast and take off in a clearance only to find that a few minutes later the weather closes in on them. But Simon is no sucker. Shortly after the sun appeared, the increase in temperature stirred up turbulence and caused the cloud base to lower and the fog to thicken again. No one was surprised when the sun gave up the unequal struggle. Conditions rapidly deteriorated and were soon well below those required for Hawk operations.

To say Brian Barrett was disappointed would be an understatement, but Simon promised that, should a suitable opportunity occur later in the year, the flypast of the train would be set up again. As Brian was changing back out of his flying equipment into his civilian clothes, a few miles away in Weston-super-Mare, his Account Manager was walking down the aisle with Annie. For once, Kelvin's mobile phone was switched off, so he had no idea that the flypast did not take place.

Flypasts

'Trying to find one small church in Central London in murky conditions is like trying to find the proverbial needle in a haystack,' said Simon as he gloomily surveyed the Met forecast just before briefing.

The flypast over St Paul's Church in Covent Garden was to be flown as the congregation left the church at the end of a memorial service to the late-Goon, Michael Bentine CBE, in recognition of his lifetime's support for RAF charities. The weather looked set to cause the flypast to be cancelled; low cloud and poor visibility in the London area was forecast to clear only very slowly to the north.

The route for the run in was very similar to that used by airliners heading for Heathrow's RW28. Anyone who has looked out of an airliner's window as it passes over London will realise the scale of the problem. It does not help that the Red Arrows are nine aircraft in close formation and that they are flying at 400 mph. Simon made the decision to go just 30 minutes before take off.

'If the weather drops below five clicks visibility or 1,500ft cloud base before we enter the London terminal area, we'll turn round and get out of there,' briefed Simon. 'Once we're committed over central London, this is the one occasion when I'll tell you to press on if you have an aircraft problem.'

Every contingency, even the worst possible one, a complete engine failure over the built-up area that is central London, has to be considered. The Red Arrows never leave anything to chance. Having to shut down the Hawk's Rolls-Royce Adour engine in flight is a very rare occurrence. If a pilot is contemplating a controlled ejection he will always look for a safe place to point the aircraft before baling out. Ian Smith had to make such a decision on final to approach to Scampton following his bird strike. There are a surprisingly large number of parks in London which might look inviting but who knows how many people there are in those parks? There is, however, Old Father Thames out on the port side running more or less parallel to track on the run in to Covent Garden.

'If the worst comes to the worst, point the aircraft into the river just before you eject,' said Simon. In the event, conditions did not drop below Simon's minima of 1,500 ft cloud base and five kilometres horizontal visibility and all the aircraft performed normally. The flypast was spot on over St Paul's Church and the timing was impeccable. The patriotic red, white and blue smoke, switched on near Chigwell just before reaching Covent

those interested in statistics, the route from brakes off at Cranwell to overhead the Church was 22 minutes 12 seconds via Stansted; the return route from overhead St Paul's Church to the break at Cranwell via Buckingham Palace was 18 minutes 45 seconds. Less than an hour after landing at Cranwell, the Team was airborne again to give a display over Cranwell and by then the wet, miserable conditions had arrived from London just in time to put a damper on the event.

Meanwhile, however, the *Hull Daily Mail* reported another satisfied customer. Pensioner Mrs Doreen Lester, who has lived all her life in Withernsea, not far from Spurn Point, one of East Yorkshire's most remote coastal spots, had never seen the Red Arrows. She challenged the Team to give her a flypast and they were able to oblige one day when they were on their way to a public display in Scotland.

'They were bang on time,' said Doreen, who was gobsmacked, according to the *Hull Daily Mail*. 'It was amazing to think they did it just for me. I think they must have nerves of steel. You could see the pilots' faces as they went over. We should all be very proud of them.'

There was another blow for the Team in early June. Gary Waterfall climbed up the side of his aircraft at Brize Norton to place his maps in the cockpit. Having done that, he somehow managed to lose his footing. His left flying boot was trapped in the spring-loaded step on the side of the airframe and he fell heavily to the ground, wrenching the whole of his leg before he fell free. At first he thought the damage was minimal and he flew back to Cranwell shortly afterwards. However, in the next 24 hours the pain, particularly in his left knee, became unbearable. The RAF doctor at Cranwell immediately referred Gary to a specialist at the Peterborough Hospital

Garden, was continued until the formation turned right over Buckingham Palace for the return to base. How many Londoners looked up with pride? How many tourists looked up in admiration? No one knows. The *Guardian* described the flypast as 'audacious'; *The Times* called it 'perfect'.

The first of many phone calls received at RAFAT HQ immediately after the flypast and before the Reds had landed back at Cranwell, came from the family of Michael Bentine thanking the Team. The next call was from the Team's own Commander-in-Chief who had been at the Service representing the Chief of the Air Staff. For

and it was decided that an operation was essential.

The operation was carried out and Gary was told, after he recovered from the anaesthetic, that the damage was more serious than had been expected.

'The specialist told me I would be off flying for at least three months,' recounted Gary. 'I told him I wanted to be fit to fly in three weeks. Realistically, it looks as though I'll not be able to fly for a couple of months.'

Predictably, Gary got absolutely no sympathy from the rest of the Team. He was now the subject of the type of banter doled out to Richie Matthews earlier in the season when he was suffering with his sinuses. The accident gave Simon a major problem to deal with. The busiest part of the season was upon them and the display would have to be changed quite significantly.

'We have a well thought out plan to cater for any of the aircraft missing on a day-to-day basis,' said Simon. 'We practice it from time to time during the winter and in Akrotiri. In the early part of the winter, before the first nine-ship, we do it all the time. However, when someone is going to be out for any length of time, we have to think about changing the show slightly to try and make it more symmetrical and to minimise the visual effect. We can't fly with a gap in the Red 3 slot; not only would it look awful but it would leave Red 5 with no one to formate on. Some shapes, EFA for example, look hopeless with one missing, so we substitute Spear which looks perfectly symmetrical.'

Simon discussed the problem at a CAG with the rest of the pilots. CAG is another acronym from the Red Arrows' vocabulary. No one is very certain what the letters stand for, 'commander's action group' and 'calling all guys' are a couple of suggestions, but it matters not; a CAG is an informal squadron discussion where everyone can have his say.

'In the first half I'll take Dave Stobie out of his Red 7 slot in the stem and move him into the Red 3 slot – which is where he was last year,' decided the Boss.

'That'll be my third time in the 3 slot,' grinned Dave, referring back to the tour of the Far East and Australia when he stood in at very short notice to replace the 1995 Red 3, Sean Perrett, who had been badly injured in a road accident in Langkawi. In the 1996 Team, Dave was Red 3 in his own right.

'You should be able to hack it this time then,' bantered someone from the back of the room.

'Apollo is fine – just the back man missing, no need for any change there,' continued Simon, ignoring the interruptions. 'The back man is missing from Diamond, but there's nothing we can do about that. The five-four cross will become a four-four cross – and to make it look neat, instead of having a lop-sided chevron at the front, we'll put Red 4 into the box.'

The discussion continued. There would have to be cosmetic changes to the sequence of coloured smoke throughout the display but the second half would need very few positional changes. The most important factor, as always, would be flight safety and escape manoeuvres.

The first appearance of the new eight-ship formation was at the Queen's Birthday Flypast over London on 14 June. The Red Arrows brought up the rear of a large formation which included aircraft representing most of the operational types in service. The formation flown was Eight Arrow, three either side of the Leader and Red 6 in his customary position line astern. The flypast was shown live on several TV channels. One commentator enthused, 'And here come the nine Red Arrows, flying in direct from their base at Marham in Norfolk.' He was, of course, wrong on both counts.

The Eight Arrow formation looked superb. Watching the television pictures of the Royal Family on the balcony of Buckingham Palace, you could see how they became much more animated as the Team approached. The Queen Mother gestured excitedly towards the Queen alongside; perhaps the Team's Commandant-in-Chief was the only one to notice that there were eight not nine aircraft.

Later that day the Team displayed at Biggin Hill.

The Manager, in his commentary, told the crowd what had happened to Gary Waterfall. Inevitably, that led to dramatic stories in the national press the following day, but BBC Radio Lincolnshire was, once again, the first to break the news.

A number of flypasts scheduled to be flown on transit flights were cancelled during June and July because of the poor summer weather but one flypast that did take place was on 16 July just south of Aberdeen. The Team had performed over Aberdeen harbour on the evening of 15 July at the start of the Tall Ships' Race. Returning to base the following day the Team flew over the Virgin Trains' Red Arrows as it passed along the rocky cliffs just south of the city en route for Plymouth. Brian Barrett, the Chief Executive, was on board Simon Meade's aircraft and thoroughly enjoyed seeing his train from a loftier viewpoint than normal. By the time the Hawks landed at Cranwell at 10.10 am the train was still north of Dundee.

White Feather

'We have ministerial approval for the tours,' announced Simon at one of the regular meetings of the Squadron executives. Earlier in the year the Team had been invited to take part in the Dubai Air Show in the United Arab Emirates and the Langkawi International Maritime and Aeronautical Exhibition 97 (LIMA97) in Malaysia, but approval had been delayed following the change of government. Now that approval had been given, detailed planning could begin in earnest. As in 1995-6, costs would be borne by British industry not the tax-payer.

John Howard, the Adjutant, had already made provisional arrangements with Embassies and High Commissions along the way and started booking hotel accommodation. Now John Leonard, Joanne Midgley and Nick Johns in the admin office had to get down to the complicated and time-consuming task of obtaining visas for some 60 Squadron personnel. The two engineering officers would have to work out where, and how, to pre-position the bulky equipment that might be needed along the route. Upstairs in the flight planning room, Tim Smith and Andy Foxhall had to start ordering the hundreds of maps, charts and airfield information documents that would be needed.

Mike Williams had the preferred route, little different from the one used in 1995, already mapped out. There would be transit night stops in Italy, Crete, Saudi Arabia, the United Arab Emirates, Pakistan, India and Thailand on the way to and from the holiday island of Langkawi off the north west coast of Malaysia. Fortunately the timing of the two air shows, Dubai in mid-November and Langkawi in the first week of December, was such that it was easy to combine both events into one long round trip consisting of 28 transit flights plus at least 16 public displays and practice displays, and lasting a total of 42 days.

As soon as word of the proposed routes began to filter out through diplomatic missions, requests began to come in for displays in countries through which the Team intended only to transit. It is sometimes quite difficult to explain, without giving offence, why, having travelled several thousands of miles, the Team cannot always fit an extra public display into their very tight schedule. Even one additional night stop disrupts the diplomatic clearances and hotel plot for the rest of the route.

'This tour means that the 1997 season will not really end until we get back to Cranwell on 20 December,' said Simon. 'The three pilots leaving at the end of the season, Tim Couston, Richie Matthews and Sean Perrett will all have their tours extended – I haven't heard any complaints yet about that. The FFNGs will have less time than normal to get up to speed for the 1998 season. Of course, by way of compensation, they will join the Squadron in September, as usual, and fly with us to Malaysia and back. On some of the transits they will have to fly in the back of the Hercules – good experience for them – on other sectors and on most displays they will fly in the Hawk back seats gaining experience.'

The wives and children will have to manage without their husbands and fathers for another six weeks and, what's more, the men will miss most of the Christmas shopping, although not all of them see that as a disadvantage.

But the winter tour seemed a long way in the future as the summer display season progressed. June was officially the wettest June for 137 years. Only six full looping displays were flown, the lowest total for many years; 13 other displays had to be restricted to either the rolling or flat variants. Three displays were cancelled altogether by the organisers because of the weather, always a heartbreaking decision to make after many months of hard work. A display at Goodwood was flown in the minimum acceptable weather conditions, but 80,000 spectators, including King Hussein of Jordan, watched enthusiastically as the Red Arrows brightened their day. The local show, just up the road at Waddington right at the end of June, seemed likely to be washed out altogether, but on each of the two mornings the clouds rolled back, the sun shone brightly and the flying displays went ahead as planned. Sadly, many people did not bother to turn out, probably put off by adverse weather forecasts, and so gate receipts were well down.

On 1 July XX264, the aircraft badly damaged in Ian Smith's bird strike, took to the air again for the first time since January. The first flight was an air test flown by Dick Johnston. As part of the test he had to invert the aircraft and apply negative g to see if any loose objects had become lodged out of sight. One tiny piece of Perspex floated into view and Dick deftly caught it. The only other extraneous object found during the flight was a single white bird's feather, which was duly presented to Smithy as a memento of his experience.

On 21 July, 41 days after his accident, Gary

Waterfall was declared fit to fly by the Senior Medical Officer at Cranwell.

'My knee was hurting more this morning than it has done for several days,' confessed Gary after the inspection. A couple of hours later he was airborne with Sean Perrett for a check ride – mandatory because he had not flown in the preceding 28 days. Two days later the full Team flew three practice sorties to get everyone back into currency and the first nine-ship public display was at Lowestoft on 24 July.

The Team was scheduled to give a display at Ostend in late July, but the Air Show there was cancelled following a tragic accident the day before when a small, piston-engined aircraft crashed into the crowd killing the Jordanian pilot and several spectators. A display at Sanicole in eastern Belgium, in which the Belgian authorities had particularly requested the Red Arrows' participation, did go ahead, even although Simon had been ready to cancel the show as a mark of respect. En route to Sanicole, the Red Arrows made a straight flypast over the show ground at Ostend as their tribute to the dead and injured.

The Red Arrows' pilots, like pilots the world over, take a keen and professional, but not morbid, interest in all flying accidents. As one of the Red Arrows said, 'The day you start brooding about accidents is the day to give up flying.' The media, inevitably, tried to predict the findings of the Belgian Board of Inquiry even before it had been set up and some media commentators suggested that this latest air show accident presaged the end of air displays altogether. But the only connection between the sad accident at Ostend and display flying such as that performed by the Red Arrows is the fact that flying machines were involved.

When the Team returned to base from Belgium there was a champagne reception waiting on the flight line for one of the Circus. Junior Technician Dave Webster joined the Team in 1994 and had been flying with the Circus since January 1996. The transit flight from Kleine Brogel brought his flying hours' total up to exactly 200.

'200 hours on type and still not gone solo,' quipped one of the pilots.

'I've never had a minute's worry,' replied Webbo in answer to a question. 'The most memorable trip was the one when we arrived at low level over Sydney Harbour.'

For some weeks in July the main taxiway at Cranwell was closed for re-surfacing. That added several minutes to the overall times for each sortie, but once that work was completed a more serious inconvenience was upon them – re-surfacing of the main runway. From the end of July until the end of September all Red Arrows' flying operations were transferred to Coningsby. Dick Johnston and Dave Chowns had been to many planning meetings at both Cranwell and Coningsby during the summer months making all the necessary arrangements. Now the pilots and ground crew were faced with long road journeys across the Lincolnshire Fens before and after every home-based sortie.

Each year the Team spend a lot of time operating from Exeter Airport because it is a very convenient stepping off point for a number of displays in the west and south. The airport authorities are always delighted to have the Team operating from their patch, even though the large numbers of sightseers tend to choke the narrow access roads leading from the A30 to the airport. This year Walkabout Film and Television, an independent film company based in Bovey Tracey, was commissioned by West Country TV to make two 30-minute documentaries about Red Arrows' operations in and around Exeter. The RAF Engineering Authority gave permission for one of the latest small digital television cameras to be mounted inside the cockpit of the Hawk and another in a rearward-facing pod underneath the aircraft. Some stunning, high definition air-to-air film was obtained. The programmes are due to be transmitted before the end of 1997, hopefully on all the ITV stations, and it is hoped to produce a video later for public sale.

People sometimes ask why the Red Arrows take a week's leave every year in the middle of August. When they went on leave on 10 August, they had flown some 50 flying sorties in the previous 40 days and they were all in need of a rest. On their return to work, they had five weeks of the European display season remaining and the prospect of the long trek out to Malaysia to look forward to.

By this time, the Adjutant was making arrangements for kitting out the FFNGs and the new ground crew personnel, and already the PRO was getting requests from the media for interviews with them. Reds 6, 8 and 9 had learned of their next postings. Sean will be returning to Wittering to fly Harriers again; Richie will return to Coltishall for another tour flying Jaguars. Tim will be going to Wittering to learn to fly the Harrier – a new experience for him.

Even before one Red Arrows' year was over, the next one was beginning and the whole sequence would start all over again.

Epilogue

The Red Arrows' 33rd European display season was typical only in the sense that there is no such thing as a typical season. Frustration was caused by aircraft unserviceabilities in the early part of the training season, many cancellations due to poor weather, and the need to operate 20 miles away from their home base for two months while the Cranwell runways were being re-surfaced. Disappointment featured large for the two pilots who spent lengthy periods off flying due to sickness. There was elation on the day of the first nine-ship formation and on Red Suit Day, especially for the first year pilots, but also for all nine display pilots on those days when they knew that they had put on an exceptionally good display. Only the Reds can savour the supreme satisfaction that comes at the end of a well-nigh perfect sortie flown in front of a crowd of several hundred thousand adoring fans. Those who work closely with the Team cannot share the pilots' elation, but can feel pride at being part of the world's premier Aerobatic Display Team, The Red Arrows.

It would have been unfair to ask Squadron Leader Simon Meade, a very modest man, to answer Michael Aspel's question about the hard act he had to follow, but the Commandant of the Central Flying School, Air Commodore Gavin Mackay, was happy to oblige, and he has the last word.

'Over the past year, my role as the Red Arrows' senior supervisor has involved me in just about every aspect of their operations. I've watched the show many times: in the air from every team position; shivering with the video cameraman at Display Datum on a windswept winter Scampton; fingers crossed at the shoulder of the C-in-C on PDA day in Cyprus; and ooohing and aaahing amongst summer airshow crowds. I've ferried their spare aircraft around, sat in on their no-prisoners-taken debriefs, paid my share of fines for screw-ups – I've even signed a few autographs! And in everything they do, in the air and on the ground, I've seen their absolute and unrelenting commitment to excellence. That is the legacy handed on by their predecessors, and they have embraced it wholeheartedly. Simon and his Team are second to none.'